THE 7 CHURCHES
NOT IN
THE BOOK OF
REVELATION

This book was made possible by:
Alan and Sheri Vaughn
Vaughn Oilfield Services
922 CR 4990
Bloomfield, NM 87413
Please send them a note of appreciation.

THE 7 CHURCHES
NOT IN
THE BOOK OF
REVELATION

GENE MIMS

with JOHN PERRY

BROADMAN
&HOLMAN
PUBLISHERS

Nashville, Tennessee

0–8054–2455–5

Published by Broadman & Holman Publishers,
Nashville, Tennessee

Dewey Decimal Classification: 250
Subject Heading: CHRISTIAN LEADERSHIP

Scripture quotations are taken from the Holman Christian
Standard Bible, © Copyright 2000 by Holman Bible
Publishers. Used by permission.

Library of Congress Cataloging-in-Publication Data

Mims, Gene, 1950–
   The 7 churches not in the book of Revelation / Gene Mims;
   with John Perry.
      p. cm.
   ISBN 0–8054–2455–5 (pbk.)
      1. Christian leadership. 2. Pastoral theology. 3. Church.
   I. Title: Seven churches not in the book of Revelation.
   II. Perry, John, 1952– III. Title.

BV652.1 .M55 2001
250—dc21
                                                    2001025121

5 6 7 8 9 10 05 04

This book is dedicated with love:

. . . to all the pastors and church leaders who follow God and serve Him faithfully . . .

. . . to my children, Jeff and Marianne who grew up well in a pastor's home . . .

. . . to my wife, Ann, my partner in ministry for twenty eight years . . .

. . . to Bruce Wilkinson, my true friend and encourager, who told me to do this.

CONTENTS

Preface   ix

1. Revelation, or the Revenge of Chicken Kiev?   1
2. The Church You Want
   vs. the Church You Have   11
3. The Seven Churches Revealed   19
4. The University Church   27
5. The Arena Church   33
6. The Corporate Church   41
7. The Machine Church   47
8. The Family Chapel   55
9. The Legacy Church   67
10. The Community Center Church   75
11. Jason's Challenge   81
12. Back to the Calling   89

Epilogue   •   101

PREFACE

Dear Reader:

The book you hold in your hands I have written especially for you. You are a leader of the people of God in a local church. You are a God-called, set-apart-for-service, gifted, sent leader. You were placed in the greatest and most wonderful fraternity of Christian servants possible by none other than the Lord himself! What a privilege! What a life! What an honor!

What a mess!

That's right. To those of us who really know, there is often a great distance between our calling and our work. If everything we have been called to is such a privilege, then why is ministry so hard? Why is it so stressful? Why is it so demanding?

You need some answers, and that's why I have written this book. It is an attempt to help you see some basic but very important reasons why leaders have difficulties leading their churches. If you are where I am and have been, then I think you will enjoy this book.

Thank you for allowing me to have some of your precious time to discuss some of these issues. Thank you also for being faithful to the calling and ministry you have in Christ. We need you, now more than ever before.

God bless you and keep you faithful.

Gene Mims

Chapter 1

REVELATION, OR THE REVENGE OF CHICKEN KIEV?

I WAS NOT ON THE ISLE OF PATMOS. I WAS IN THE AISLE seat of a Boeing 737. And I was not in a vision mode. Actually, I was in a bad mood, trying to overcome my third airline meal of the week.

OK . . . OK . . . I'll confess if you promise never to tell. The fact is, I was under the gun big time. I was on my way to Southern California to teach a seminary class on church leadership. And seminary students have a way of seeing through the smoke and getting to the real issues—especially if you don't know what you're talking about.

I was racking my brain to find a way to explain why so many church leaders have trouble leading churches. How do you find a way to explain the root of so many conflicts and misunderstandings? But as we passed over the clouds high above the desert somewhere between New Mexico and California, it hit me like a plastic tray of chicken Kiev: churches come in a series of sizes and shapes that fit into specific, perfectly sensible categories.

And if you can figure out what category a church is in, you can figure out how to serve it as a pastor. You can also see how—or whether—your gifts and skills match a congregation's needs. What's more, identifying and understanding a church's category can relieve a vast percentage of the frustration and grief pastors feel when they're working as hard and faithfully as they can, but just can't seem to connect with their congregations.

But what categories? What are they, and where do they come from?

DIFFERENT WAYS OF WORSHIP

As I sat there flying into the sunset, waiting for my body to digest the mystery meat du jour I had just eaten, I began thinking about the fact that the body of Christ is as unique in its parts as the family of humankind. We are many and varied, which explains so much of why we worship, witness, and minister in such different ways. The churches that gather weekly for Great Commission causes are different yet similar. Most have some dominant characteristics that they share with other congregations, but other features are shared only with churches that embrace the same priorities and worship styles.

So somewhere between an announcement for unexpected turbulence and a rough landing, which awoke me from my inspirational slumber, I saw them:

The Seven Churches Not *in the Book of Revelation!*

"THAT EXPLAINS EVERYTHING!"

I want to issue a quick disclaimer here. What I am about to share with you is not to be taken exactly as new revelation. There is humor here if I have communicated correctly. Laughing out loud is OK. And there will be times when you say to yourself, "Yes, that's it! That's the church of my childhood!" or, "That explains everything about where I pastor/serve/attend now!"

I also hope you begin to get some insight into how diverse but predictable congregations can be. This is normal, and no one kind is superior to another. There are Great Commission Christians in all kinds of churches.

My greatest desire, however, is to encourage you as a leader to understand your people and to understand your own leadership style. This will allow you to make the necessary adjustments—and give yourself enough time—to become a great leader.

If I have done my job well you will:

- be encouraged to love your people for who they really are,

- understand what it takes to develop a New Testament church,
- be patient in serving where you are and not give up,
- take joy in who you are in God's plan,
- have a few good laughs.

Now let's take a look at what an airline meal—and the pressure of a seminary class—can really do.

A FAMILIAR STORY

Jason Benson has been in his first pastorate for nearly eighteen months now and something doesn't feel quite right. He can't put his finger on what is bothering him, but it's there and it won't go away. He is improving in his skills as a pastor and preacher. His people seem to respond to him, especially when he visits them in the local hospital or around town. They also seem to appreciate his pulpit ability. He studies hard and wants to learn and communicate everything he can to his folks each week.

But something doesn't feel quite right . . .

Jason doesn't know it yet, but he is about to go through an awakening. It has nothing to do with his theology or his skills as a preacher. It has nothing to do with his training or calling to ministry. It has everything to do with the discovery of what kind of church he pastors and what kind of leader he seems destined to be.

Jason is about to enter conflict for which he has no preparation. It is a conflict every pastor faces, and it is necessary in order to grow and develop as an effective leader. This conflict will help Jason get in touch with the reality that seminary cannot give him: the reality which may surprise him, disappoint him, and frustrate him, but which will eventually center his life in effective ministry.

You see, the church Jason pastors is not actually the church he wants, nor is it the church he thinks it is. Jason has been to seminary and studied the New Testament. He has learned what he thinks a church is like when the Lord is working. He left seminary loaded with church growth books. He can articulate principles, purposes, diagrams, and even resources on what it takes to grow a church. He has even attended conferences in California, Tennessee, and Illinois on church issues. He is ready. But the fact is, he is *not* ready—not even close yet—for what he is about to experience.

His assumptions do not yet match the expectations and experience of his people. They see themselves and their church one way, and Jason sees them differently. They are comfortable being a small group of committed Christians while Jason wonders why they do not see how many persons live around them who are unchurched and unreached. The field is ripe for harvest, but nobody wants to grab a scythe and get to work.

BIG PLANS, BIG FRUSTRATIONS

When he came in for the interview, Jason said all the right things and so did the committee. It was a marriage made over steak and potatoes at one of the nicer restaurants in town. They talked about leadership, ministries, programs, and vision. All the right words were said; all the courtship was proper. Nobody got out of line. Nobody spoke in an untoward way.

In fact, nobody talked about anything but the previous pastor and what he couldn't or didn't do.

There was a lot of hope and optimism. They talked about Jason's views on evangelism and worship. As Jason talked, the committee would nod in unison. "Yes," they would say, "yes, that's the kind of man we need here." Then they would talk about worship and Jason would say how he wanted God just to come and meet them in worship and how so many new things were being done in worship to help people. "Yes," they would say in unison, rocking back and forth, "yes, yes, yes."

Eighteen months later nothing has really changed at this new church. The things Jason feels his people don't seem to understand. They don't seem to be quite as excited as he is about those choruses he'd like to introduce. They can't quite memorize them, they say, or they don't know the words, or it's a little too loud—and where did that canned music come from anyway? Can't Mamie Sue play the piano like she always has? Jason doesn't quite understand. They agree with him that something needs to be done but never get around to dealing with what to do first.

Jason finally concludes that all his people are for him they just don't seem to be *with* him.

THE CHURCH WE WANT

Does Jason's experience sound or feel familiar? I remember an amazing experience preaching one time in the hills of East Tennessee. After the congregation had taken the service away from me by doing the Jericho march right around the building in the middle of my sermon—to my chagrin and the interruption of my well-prepared homiletical discourse—a man came up at the end of the crying and the boo-hooing and the altar call to say, "Preacher I want you to know, tonight I had a feeling." (For those of you who don't know, a Jericho march is when the entire congregation gets up and marches in a circle around the sanctuary several times.)

I had a feeling too, and I wasn't at all sure I liked it.

Do you have a knot in your stomach right now thinking about where you serve or attend? Have you recently felt that same uneasiness Jason feels? You know something is brewing and it's not quite right but you can't put your finger on it. In thirty years of ministry, I have experienced and observed this frequently.

If you do not clearly understand your church and its people, and clearly recognize your own leadership traits, then trouble will find you. When it does, you can be discouraged and even doubtful of your ability and calling. You might leave your congregation too soon, hoping to find a better fit somewhere. I have learned this about that: you can only serve the people as they really are. You cannot pretend that they are something they are not.

THE GOOD NEWS

As uneasy as you might feel about all this right now, let me give you some hope. There is a way through this and it begins with understanding—an understanding of

The Seven Churches Not *in the Book of Revelation.*

Back to my airplane story for a moment. I knew the seminary students I was going to meet would be ready for me to give them some wisdom and help in understanding the nature of churches, and on how to give those churches the effective leadership they require.

If you know anything about today's seminary students, you know they come ready for action. None of this theory-only, listen-to-the-expert stuff. No way! These men and women come ready to challenge you and take every one of your thoughts captive to their own opinions. As I mulled over what we needed to discover during the class, I knew that "oughts," "shoulds," and "maybes" would not do. Besides, I kept telling myself, these people need something real to hang on to. By itself, identifying the nature of the church would not be enough, although that would certainly be a starting point. We needed something more. We needed something fresh.

I needed something fresh!

So I did what any red-blooded Evangelical bureaucrat would do under such stress: I had a vision. Well all right, maybe it wasn't really a vision, but it was an experience. No one can take an experience away from you—so I felt safe. Actually, I think well under pressure sometimes, and this stuff had been circulating in my brain for a long time.

In fact, it was just over fifteen years ago . . .

NOTHING'S WORSE THAN NOTHING

Pastoring a large congregation had been one of my overt desires for most of my ministry. Well, I finally got one, and it was and is a good one. But, like Jason, I began to get this nagging feeling that something wasn't quite right. I had been there for several years, and on the surface everything was fine. In fact it was almost too good (you pastors out there know what I'm talking about).

I began to notice a leveling off of interest in some of the things that I really enjoyed. For instance, when I talked about volunteer missions a few brave souls would sign up for the trips and go. When I talked about evangelism a few persons would enroll in our training courses. But when I talked about being salt and light, about holiness, stewardship, worship, and prayer, the response was always the same. Nothing. And I mean nothing.

Now every preacher will tell you that no response is not only dangerous, it's unhealthy. Even though I've never seen the numbers, I am firmly convinced that more pastors die from lack of response than any other reason. It kills you and you can't fix it. I found myself preaching the right stuff (in short sermons too!) to good people (I loved them) for all the right reasons, but with no visible effect.

I became increasingly frustrated to the point where I finally said once in a sermon, "I feel like a man who sees a house on fire and rushes to tell the people inside to get out, and they thank him for coming by and explain they will leave as soon as the TV program they are watching is over."

That is a very in-your-face kind of thing to say to a large group of people present along with a live radio and television audience, don't you think? I thought after the words left my mouth, *I've done it this time. My goose is cooked.*

You know what kind of response I had? Nothing. *Nada, zip, zero!* What kind of response is nothing anyway? No anger, disappointment, sympathy, understanding? Nothing. And we all know nothing is worse than nothing.

KNOWING WHAT'S IMPORTANT

I went back to the drawing board and came up with a novel idea. I formed a committee and we hired a human relations consulting firm to come in with one assignment: find out what is important to these people I serve as pastor.

The consultants came and they met with groups, individuals, committees. They met with young people, with old people, with leaders, staff members, softball teams (I'm not lying—besides I was desperate), and even a few people who were not in our church. They left and then returned a few weeks later with several large spiral-bound volumes. That impressed us because we didn't know that large spiral-bound notebooks are what consultants are really paid to do.

I'm getting off track here.

We had a private meeting and that's where my life changed as a leader.

I won't go into details, but suffice it to say that what I learned was that I really did not know my church. I discovered that our people cared about the Great Commission as much as I did. They cared about growing as much as I did. They cared about our location and our future as much as I did. But the way I wanted to shape the church and do ministry was very different from their expectations. We all wanted the same things, but we had very different ideas about how to do them. I woke up and realized that the church I wanted and thought I had was in fact very different from the church I actually pastored.

Chapter 2

THE CHURCH YOU WANT VS. THE CHURCH YOU HAVE

ONE OF THE BIGGEST REASONS MINISTERS ARE disappointed and unfulfilled today is that we want a church we don't have, or have a church we don't want. The cause of that kind of mismatch is simple: everybody has an idea about what a church is, but very few people lead, attend, or know that kind of church.

What did the consulting firm we hired tell me? Well, they told me for instance that my church was a church where relationships meant everything. We were running about a thousand in Sunday School at that time, and about 1,300 in worship. I thought I was in a church that needed a leader to set a vision. I thought I was a visionary leader.

I found out instead that most of the people in our church thought the pastoral ministries—which were the ministries of yours truly—basically stunk. Forty-four percent of the people in the survey said, "We don't think pastoral ministry is very strong here." I don't know where you sit, but that's not a very good opinion to hear when you're the pastor. And 44 percent of the people think you're not getting the job done! What I eventually discovered—to my relief—was that they did want to do what I wanted to do, but in a different way.

LOOKING FOR THE PERFECT CHURCH

We all know of a church we would like to have. It's usually in another part of the city, or even another part of the country, and seems in every way to be just what we want. We have heard of the ministries, the preaching, and the commitment of the laypeople. Everything seems to be ideal over there—until we talk to the pastor! To our surprise we find him frustrated and searching for just the right combination to become the perfect church.

Several things are at play here. First, we have to understand that churches are not static and inert. Even the church that seems to change the least is really a changing church. People change, families change, and therefore churches change. It is impossible to find the perfect church unless we are willing to change with it.

Second, most of what a perfect church would be exists only in our minds, and is usually imagined according to what would fit our own selfish needs and desires. Churches exist, period. There are large ones, small ones, wealthy ones, active ones, old ones, and new ones. Finding the perfect one is simply not possible.

Third, we generally take our understanding of what a perfect church should be from our understanding of the New Testament church. The problem with this, however, is that there is no such thing as *the* New Testament church. There were many churches in the first century, and none of them was perfect. There was the young church in Jerusalem that had problems feeding some widows. There was Corinth where things got out of control. There was Thessalonica where some folks stopped working. How about the seven churches in Revelation, or those in Galatia? None was perfect, but they were all New Testament churches.

THE DANGEROUS PATH OF CHANGE

The perfect church is not to be found. But that's not to say that a church cannot be better or do more. Let's go back to our young pastor friend Jason again for a moment.

Jason is increasingly frustrated because nothing seems to work as he seeks to move his church along the dangerous path of change. I say dangerous path of change because at this point he is unaware of some dynamics about his church that may cause him some damage if he continues on the particular path he has chosen.

At the same time Jason cannot exactly describe what he is looking for in a church, he is overlooking some very important realities in his congregation. He has not read *The Seven Sins of a Young and Ambitious Pastor*. The reason is simple: no one would dare write such a thing! It's too risky, painful, and potentially harmful. To expose such secrets would be professional suicide. Never mind that, however. I will give them to you here only if you remember that Jason is a *fictional* character and that his church is a *fictional* congregation. Any resemblance to any real pastor or church is purely coincidence. (Don't blame me. Remember, I'm just making this stuff up!)

SEVEN PASTORAL SINS

Sin #1: Not accepting people for who they are

Jason is overlooking the fact that the only people he can work with are the people he actually has. Who they are and what they are will not be easy to change. There are life patterns and years of believing things about themselves and their church that will not go away quietly like the morning dew. Jason often dreams about the church he wants: a church filled with evangelistic people who give sacrificially of themselves, their time, money, and talents. They listen with rapt attention to every word he speaks and move at every command.

Wake up, Jason! This is the real church world. This is a world filled with old people who formed opinions about the kingdom of God long before you were born. They are steeped in a culture that no longer exists. They built their houses in 1940 and can't imagine why you want to live on God's little half-acre out there in a $350,000 house. They don't get it. They eat everything out of cans. They don't throw anything away. Combined with them are their children and grandchildren, who live in today's world with a faith that is new, forming, and not yet tested. Do not overlook who your people really are before you try to make them into something you want them to be.

Sin #2: Believing that preaching will change them

Jason has begun to labor under the mistaken notion that if he preaches well enough people will change. He'll study more, he'll preach longer, he'll preach less, he'll be creative, he'll be traditional. He is trying to change their lives by changing their minds. He is sure new sermons on old themes will be just the thing. But he's forgotten what he learned in seminary about how much people retain from an audio experience. He will have to preach many times on many things for his people to remember even the basics of what he said. They don't remember his first sermon. They don't remember that he labored all week for thirty or forty hours (or so he said) to preach this knockout sermon on the kingdom of God and the vision he has for Harmony Fellowship out here in Ruralville. They actually cannot remember from one week to the next much of what he said, so how can they internalize what he means?

Wake up, Jason! Preaching is important, but it is important only in connection with the rest of what a pastor and church do. Jason was told in seminary that preaching is the most important thing a pastor does. No, Jason, it's the most important thing in preaching class, but it's not all that big a deal to Grandma and Grandpa out there in the pew. This is the real world, and people hear, read, and see all kinds of things. There

is no shortage of thoughts, philosophies, and ideas—
competing thoughts, philosophies, and ideas. People are
exposed to thousands of these every day of their lives.
Preaching is a powerful mechanism for change, but only
over a long period of time.

Sin #3: Assuming everyone wants to change

Jason has begun to labor under an appealing but erro-
neous idea. (I hate to write such stuff, but remember this
is *fictional*.) He actually thinks people *want* their church
to change and be different, because he forgot they were
so happy with their church the way it was when he came
there. What they were unhappy with was the preacher
they booted out. Jason has spoken with a few of the
leaders, and they even told him some changes were
needed. They talked about growth and even the possibil-
ity of a new building. (After all, they built one thirty
years ago, didn't they?) They like when Jason speaks of
the future because they want to know what he sees.

Wake up, Jason! Talk is cheap, and it is infinitely easier to talk than to change. Most people in churches have
no intention of changing. Why would they want to
change when they like their Sunday School class, prayer
group, and friends? Why would they want to mess with
the power structure, finances, and organization? Why
would they want to upset what it has taken them years
to develop and enjoy? Talk about change all you want,
just don't try it.

You get the idea. We'll move along a little faster now.

Sin #4: Believing the few represent the many

Jason has surrounded himself (or has been surrounded) with three or four individuals who encourage
him to make changes. They are with him in every way.
They appreciate the direction he wants to move. They

like his style and understand clearly what he says. But they do not represent the whole of the congregation. There are always a few persons who see the need for change in their church and want to see it happen. They will support the pastor and encourage him. But this is not a consensus or a representative sample of the entire congregation.

Sin #5: Expecting worship to accelerate the change

Jason is one of a growing number of pastors who define change as it begins with worship. Nearly every church that calls a pastor has issues to settle with worship. Worship is not the place to start making the changes that churches need. They need purpose, vision, and biblical foundations to be developed or restored first. Jason likes a certain style of music and worship and assumes that change will come best, fastest, and easiest if the worship style is changed to conform to his preferences. He cannot realize that most people think very little about worship, and that if changes in worship style are perceived in their minds as personal criticism of them, their preferences, and their traditions, then trouble is sure to follow.

Sin #6: Believing an expert will convince them

Jason has attended several conferences on church health and growth. He has read books on it and had conversations with fellow ministers. He has listened to tapes, watched videos, logged onto Web sites, and even corresponded with some leading pastors in this area. He is excited about what can happen if his church gets the vision for growth. In his desire to see his church grow he has purchased various studies and guides on growth, conducted training classes for his leadership, and brought in a person recognized as an expert in the field.

To his surprise and disappointment, however, his people have been only mildly receptive to any idea of change in the church program or style.

Sin #7: Imitating another pastor

Jason is young and eager to become a good pastor. He has looked around and found a man to imitate. He watches him lead his church successfully and wants to do the same. He has begun to speak like him in meetings and even when he preaches. He has taken on a different tone in conversations with church leaders. Without realizing it he has changed his natural style for an alien one that doesn't really suit him or take advantage of his gifts. It is not working, and he senses that without realizing what has happened or knowing exactly what to do about it.

If Jason does not get some insight and perspective soon, he will likely make another grave mistake. It's one that is made all too often by well-meaning pastors of every age, and can begin a cycle of uncertainty in a pastor's life and career that is very difficult to break.

It is the greatest mistake of all: the mistake of believing that the *next* church will be the *right* church.

Chapter 3

THE SEVEN CHURCHES REVEALED

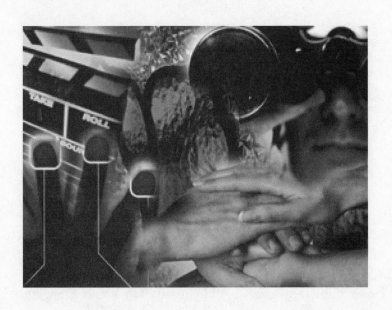

IF HE WERE TO CHANGE CHURCHES AGAIN, JASON would probably just be trading one set of conflicts and misunderstandings for another. If he doesn't deal with his pastoral challenges here, he'll face them somewhere else down the road. But before we blame Jason for being too naive or ambitious in thinking a new pastorate will be the solution to his problems, let's stop to think about what he's up against. The sheer number of variables is almost overwhelming. No wonder there's a survival instinct inside somewhere saying, "Run!"

Look at the list below and consider what it's like to pastor a congregation you hardly know. (You may have some firsthand experience with this already!) Just some of the main potential variables include:

1. Size—Large, Medium, Small
2. Style of Worship—Reflective, Structured, Passionate
3. Geography—Urban, Suburban, Rural
4. Economic Condition—Wealthy, Moderate, Poor
5. Social Standing—Professional, Working Class, Needy
6. Education—College, High School, Grade School, Illiterate
7. Political—Liberal, Moderate, Conservative
8. Theological—Liberal, Moderate, Conservative, Fundamental
9. Denominational—Independent, Loosely Aligned, Aligned

Is it no wonder that Jason is in a spin? He doesn't know what he has, how it behaves, or what to do about anything that comes up. He doesn't know that changing pastorates probably won't help him. He doesn't know the secrets of the Seven Churches *Not* in the Book of Revelation!

THE MOST IMPORTANT VARIABLE

When you take the twenty-nine different choices listed under the nine variables above, the combinations are almost endless. And that's only the beginning. Jason could be the leader of a small, structured, suburban, moderately wealthy, professional, reasonably educated, politically conservative, fundamental, independent church and still not know everything he needs to know about his congregation or how to lead it!

Let us add another even bigger dimension to the list above: What *type* or *style* of church are you in? This is the most important question of all because there are seven possibilities that made up my vision, and together those seven are descriptive of every church known to mankind. (OK, I'm using hyperbole, but it's important because I'm trying to keep you interested.)

Anyway, to know these seven types of churches is to love them. I saw them clearly on my flight to California. Or maybe I should say in my vision of them they were obvious, but not necessarily clear at all. Every church I have ever known has a dominant characteristic that places it in one of the seven categories. Each church then has subdominant characteristics like size and worship style. Each church is dynamic and is subject to change depending on its pastor and other important factors.

I know you think I'm making this up, but we haven't even gotten to the good stuff yet. I promise you the picture will get clearer in a moment. I just want you to see how hard it is to put a finger on a church problem or opportunity. It is hard to understand who we are as pastors or lay leaders, and harder still to change, move, or lead a church.

It reminds me of what Mark Twain once said: "Everybody complains about the weather, but no one does anything about it." We often fret or worry about how our church is developing (or not developing), but we feel as powerless to do anything about it as we do to raise the temperature or stop the rain.

THE NATURE OF THE CHURCH

The church is so big and all-encompassing that it's almost indescribable, but there are certain truths that we can agree on:

- It is a body and a family.
- It involves people doing and being.
- It is centered in Christ but is expressed in many ways.
- It is focused on the Great Commission.
- It functions through evangelism, discipleship, fellowship, ministry, and worship.
- Its fruits are souls saved, believers transformed, ministries launched, and missions advanced.

Every church is made up of believers who are in the dynamic process of transformation. In that process are the elements of those things that we know, do, and are or become. If you ask your doctor what has made you the person you are, he's going to say, "Well, you're made up of specific cells and enzymes and chemicals, all determined by your DNA." A church has DNA too, but it's not molecules shaped like a double helix. Instead, it's a series of variables that combine to give a church its spiritual essence.

To start with, there are two consistent factors in the lives of believers that make them successful as Christians. First is the personal and spiritual relationship between one member of the congregation and another. Second is the relationship between the way one member serves the church and the way the others serve: how all the different interests and skills represented come together to form the church body.

These two factors are indispensable to understanding the nature and function of a church. In fact the words *nature* and *function* are good terms for our understanding.

Nature, as in the nature of a believer's life or a congregation's life, speaks to something given by the Holy Spirit of God. It is the nature of our spiritual lives for the Holy Spirit to produce spiritual fruit. The fruit of the Holy Spirit is the key ingredient in keeping a church a church. It provides the essence of what we need for good relationships. It is the glue that sticks us together despite our differences and opinions. It is the lubricant that helps us to function despite our wide variety of gifts and interests.

Paul knew this when he wrote,

"But the fruit of the Spirit is love, joy, peace, patience, kindness, goodness, faith, gentleness, self-control. Against such things there is no law" (Gal. 5:22–23).

Why did he write these words? To show the Galatians how to overcome the sins of the flesh. Notice how the fruit of the Spirit is relational. We often overlook this truth and internalize the fruit for our own benefit. Fruit borne by the Holy Spirit is for the benefit of everyone else. Perhaps it's a good idea to look at the works of the flesh mentioned by the apostle before the list of spiritual fruit.

"Now the works of the flesh are obvious: sexual immorality, moral impurity, promiscuity, idolatry, sorcery, hatreds, strife, jealousy, outbursts of anger, selfish ambitions, dissensions, factions, envy, drunkenness, carousing, and anything similar" (Gal. 5:19–21a).

GOOD RELATIONSHIPS

All of these words speak to relationships we can have with persons. The works of the flesh destroy relationships, and the fruit of the Spirit builds them. A church must have good relationships with the Father and among believers or nothing can be accomplished. This speaks to the *being* side of the believer's life. The metaphor for this is family. Family speaks to us of relationships. Relationships are crucial to a family or nothing else works.

There is another important dimension to a church, however, that we have to understand. The metaphor that best speaks to this is the body. In fact, if you ask one hundred believers to describe the nature of a church, 99 percent of them will say the church is either the body of Christ or the family of God.

The metaphor of the body, like the family, is a biblical one. It speaks not to the relationships between believers but to the functions those believers employ. Instead of understanding our churches and the lives of their members in *relationship* to one another, we understand our churches by what each believer *does*. What do you do in your church? How would you ever answer that question in a legitimate way? Is it possible to describe your Christian life in terms of your participation in a program or ministry?

Scripture gives us a deeper understanding than that. The Bible repeatedly speaks of our *gifts* for ministry. Every believer is a minister, called of God and given spiritual gifts for works of service. It is God's work we do as he works through us. Spiritual fruit is important because we must have the proper relationships with one another in order for the local body (the church) to function. No one has enough spiritual gifts to function for the rest of the church. It takes all the gifts God gives to his people bound together to do his will in a local church.

HELP IS ON THE WAY

No wonder Jason is confused and struggling. He has a church he doesn't know. But we can help him. If he can understand some of the above with the information in the chapters that follow, he might make it yet. He is now ready for—trumpet fanfare please!—

The Seven Churches Not *in the Book of Revelation!*

These seven churches are not in Scripture, but they are as real as the seven that *are* listed in Revelation. They have characteristics as definable as any entity we might describe. They are, in no particular order, as follows:

1. The University Church—where the emphasis is on teaching, learning, and doctrine.
2. The Arena Church—worship-centered, where performance and entertainment are key.
3. The Corporate Church—large, complex, intricate, and a model of efficiency.
4. The Machine Church—program-oriented, focused on building, missions, and task management.
5. The Family Chapel Church—based on family ties, where personal relationships come first.
6. The Legacy Church—rich in tradition, often focused on a great event or personality of the past.
7. The Community Center Church—committed to community service and local issues.

Would you like to guess some of the other character-istics of any of these right now, and compare them against the collected wisdom of yours truly, along with about fifteen seminary students? (Caution: I *am* an adjunct professor.)

By the way, this list is not the result of qualitative and quantitative research. Who needs it when you have students? Research takes too long and my publisher wouldn't spring for the costs. Remember that churches have dominant characteristics and subdominant ones. They also are dynamic, which means that churches may change over the years.

A PLACE IN GOD'S PLAN

And let me say something important as we continue here. Every one of these churches is a good church. Any one of them can be very, very effective. One isn't better than another; they're simply different, each worshiping God and fulfilling the Great Commission in its own perfectly good, perfectly acceptable way. There's something about each one that attracts me, and honestly I'd like my church to be a little bit of every one.

And now, after all this waiting, you can finally join Jason on a remarkable journey of discovery that will help you determine the kind of church you serve, the kind of leader you are, and the kind of leader you need to become.

Chapter 4

THE UNIVERSITY CHURCH

The Key: Instruction
Pastor as Professor

THE UNIVERSITY CHURCH HAS A FOCUS ON TEACHING, learning, and doctrine. Its mission is truth-taught, believed, and held at all costs. University Churches are often standard-bearers of truth in their communities and even around the world.

Picture the pastor. He is a teacher at heart. He is a professor and keeper of the truth. He reveals error and heresy. His style is pedantic (I looked it up). He is serious and skilled in the art of presentation. He lectures and calls it preaching, and he is good at it. Think of a pastor you know like him. I mean, he squeezes the Greek and Hebrew until they scream for mercy. (There's nothing else even A. T. Robertson could do when he gets finished.)

University Pastors build solid churches with solid saints who hold the truth in reverence and practice it with passion. The University Pastor can lay claim to holding the truth claims of the Bible high, so that all who hear may see those claims and follow them in God's will.

The University Church congregation is filled with learners, note takers, and those who enjoy listening to tapes of the messages. If the Christian life is "a pursuit of things we do, know, and are," then these people come down solidly in the "know" camp. They begin with knowing and move toward the other two. These folks *want to go deep*. They need to go deep. No, they *have* to go deep.

"Deep into what?" is often a good question, but I don't want to get into more trouble than I am already.

A PASSION FOR TRUTH

The University Pastor is a man who is able to study, understand, retain, and communicate truths of Scripture in a way most of us can only dream about. Hours and hours will tick by as he studies the Word of God in order to communicate to the saints the verities of God. These pastors are truly defenders of the faith and are best characterized as having passion for the truth. They may lack the communication skills of others, but when it comes to reason, reflection, and recognition of the truth, they are without peers.

The University Pastor has an affinity for discovery. He can set truth in order in a way that helps his people understand their God, their world, themselves, and how to think clearly enough to live as God desires them to live. They are masters at seeing in Scripture what others miss and finding answers to what others can only question. They are men who never waste any fruits of their study. Over a lifetime, they build one biblical truth upon another biblical truth with passion and dedication.

Their spiritual giftedness is teaching, and they are master teachers in the best sense of the word. People who long to go deep in the Word of God find great satisfaction in sitting under the teaching/preaching ministry of University Pastors. These men are doctrinally sound, spiritually right, and filled with integrity. Their passion for truth is released when they preach and teach. Many of them would fit the vivid description once used for a preacher holding forth in the pulpit: "He was truth on fire!"

Is there any doubt as to who the original University Pastor might be? The apostle Paul, without a doubt. He was a teacher from the first day of his Christian life to the last day of his time on earth. He taught believers in Ephesus for a year and a half until they were known as

"Christians" by everyone in the city. He taught faithful men to teach faithful men, knowing it was teaching that would establish believers in doctrine and practice. Every Epistle he wrote is a teaching masterpiece, filled with rich, inspired words that Christians have read and applied for centuries.

Can't you just imagine him today standing at a flannel graph showing children how Jonah was swallowed by the whale? At an overhead projector teaching the Thessalonians about the Antichrist and the Second Coming? How about in a large arena with a PowerPoint presentation? It's too much I know, but if there was ever a pastor who taught it has to be Paul. He went far but he always went deep in doctrine and practice.

I am so thankful for those pastors who keep us on track doctrinally. They, like Paul, are kingdom builders, teaching their people to think, understand, and apply the things of God in unique and effective ways.

MIND AND WILL

The University Pastor may not have some of the valuable gifts and abilities other ministers have been blessed with. He may prefer a comfortable chair in the pastor's book-lined study to stomping around the parish—or even standing in the pulpit. He will not generally motivate his people best by touching their emotions. He is best at penetrating their minds and wills. He may be too precise for some, too rational for others, and even too removed by the estimation of yet another part of the congregation. He is able to use his gifts for ministry in unique and powerful ways, but they are different gifts from those of a preacher who achieves an emotional connection.

This type of pastor generally leads by modeling a genuine lifestyle according to the truth he teaches. His influence is great as his people see his love and commitment to them as the guardian of their souls. University Pastors have great followings, and it is no surprise that they often publish their sermons and have tape ministries.

Can you think of a church like this? They come in all sorts of packages: large, small, urban, suburban. Some of the world's greatest churches are University Churches.

However . . .

Not everyone can enjoy this type of church. If you put a premium on celebration in worship, accomplishing tasks in the community, or other participatory, hands-on experiences, the University Church can be something of a challenge to endure. Who wants to sit around and "go deep" when there's work to be done? Why spend so much time studying when we could be worshiping and praising the Lord?

Well, I don't want to get off on too much of a tangent here. See the checklist below to see if you might be in—or best gifted to serve—a University Church.

CHECKLIST

__ Your pastor has self-published his teaching outlines.

__ Your pastor has sets of tapes on doctrines Christians believe.

__ Your pastor's favorite kingdom instrument is at least one of the following: an overhead projector, a Marks-a-Lot, a flipchart, PowerPoint.

__ He knew C. I. Scofield personally.

I see many churches across the nation and around the world that are University Churches. They are great bodies of great Christians, and God uses them mightily.

Chapter 5

THE ARENA
CHURCH

The Key: Experience
Pastor as Performer

THERE IS GENERALLY ONE WORD THAT DESCRIBES THE Arena Church: Wow!

These are worship-centered, experiential types of churches. Performance, experience, and entertainment are their strongest, most apparent characteristics. There is an electricity produced for the benefit of everyone in the congregation that is sometimes hard for the rest of us to take for very long. The pace is fast, exciting, exhilarating—and sometimes wild. Can you think of some right away?

These churches don't hold services—they produce weekly events. Stages are set, props are lined up, lights are strategically focused. Pulpits and choir chairs are optional—chances are nobody up there is going to have time to sit down. The cameras are ready. That's right, cameras—this is too good to go unseen! Let the action begin! It is too alive ever to be captured on radio or cassette tape. You have to see this to believe it! The key component here is experience. Nothing is more important than the experience the people have and nothing is more apparent in the services.

One sure-fire characteristic of the Arena Church is that when the service is over and the congregation leaves, they're just as tired as the pastor. And you've got to have some Kleenex up front, because for plenty of the people streaming up to the altar, the trip is serious business.

CENTER STAGE

Did I mention the pastor is always at center stage? He's the focus of the worship experience, continuously in the middle of the action. He is a tremendously gifted communicator and leader, and has great discernment about the people who fill his church as the minutes count down to airtime. He is able to look out on his congregation and determine exactly what they need in that moment. He is the major player and star in the weekly drama, working for the Lord to see him move among his people.

The Arena Pastor is truly one of the most remarkable leaders among preachers anywhere. In fact, he is often the envy of other pastors for his style, confidence, and ability to move and motivate people to do things other pastors only dream about doing. The Arena Pastor is an individual who is able to focus on people in a dimension unknown to other ministers. He takes energy from his people, from the message God has given him, and from the worship service itself. It is more than a stage, it's a forum—a place of experiential combat where the pastor's people come to be reminded of the Truth with a capital *T*.

Arena Pastors communicate the nature of God as no other pastors do. They have vivid imaginations, excellent presentation skills, and enormous passion and energy that are released and revealed when they speak. They are the proclaimers of the faith and the motivators of the faithful.

An Arena Pastor may personally be either an introvert or an extrovert, but he feels best about ministry when he's in the spotlight leading worship. He frames his identity and his church's identity in terms of the Sunday program. These pastors know the importance of people, programs, and projects, but nothing—and I mean nothing—is more important than the worship service to them. In their view, this is the arena where the Lord moves and people are visibly changed.

The worship experience is the truest indicator to them of whether they and their churches have been successful.

The service, the invitation, and the response of the people are all-important ingredients for the Arena Pastor in determining the spiritual health of the people he serves.

SPIRITUAL GIFTEDNESS

Arena Pastors have unique spiritual giftedness to sense the needs of their people and address those needs in sermons and worship. They also have a sense of what God is doing, especially during a service. These are the men who want to worship and put tons of energy into their presentations. With remarkable precision, they are able to align the needs of their people with the will of God and motivate them to seek his will for their lives.

These preachers have a natural confidence when describing the will of God and discerning the proper response for their people. It's no surprise that these men often build large congregations and raise large amounts of money for buildings, missions, and ministry. They lead people where most other ministers fear to tread.

OFFSTAGE TRANSFORMATION

Another characteristic of Arena Pastors is that they are generally quite different away from the pulpit or worship service—"offstage" as it were. They may be soft-spoken, somewhat shy, or even reclusive when they leave the church. Around their families they may change personalities completely. In public they may manifest a confident swagger, but in private they're different. One reason for this is that preaching calls for one thing, while leading, pastoring, and being a good father and husband all call for something quite different. These men are the way they are because of God's gifting them to lead the way they do.

Many people enjoy the leadership of Arena Pastors on account of the excitement and passion they radiate. Arena Pastors have an innate ability to make people feel that they are the focus of their entire attention. When you are led by an Arena Pastor, you feel that he has you in mind in everything he says and everything he does. The excitement Arena Pastors generate can be electrifying. People in that body of believers enjoy feeling the presence of God and sensing the moving of God under the leadership of their pastors.

Conversely, Arena Pastors often struggle in areas where other pastors are strongest. They may lack skills and patience for careful planning. They are often spontaneous people who lead intuitively. That means they may not spend as much time in preparation for sermons as University Pastors, for example, because they are naturally gifted communicators and they find preaching an easy calling. They're quite comfortable winging it: you don't see many clear Plexiglas pulpits with notes showing through from the other side.

For all their giftedness, Arena Pastors do not often reflect on how what they say might affect others. They are truly God's champions, and they speak with boldness and assurance that leaves debate and discussion aside. But that means that to persons inclined to process ideas before accepting them or to consider an issue before jumping in and doing it, Arena Pastors are an enigma.

THE ORIGINAL ARENA PASTORS

Two biblical characters who remind me of Arena Pastors are Elijah and Peter. Elijah confronted the prophets of Baal on Mount Carmel before the entire nation of Israel. He was unafraid of the challenge and called down fire from heaven with great drama and effect. Simon Peter was another biblical character with great boldness. His dramatic sermon at Pentecost matched his inward passion and emotion. He could move crowds and was unafraid of the arena whether he preached to thousands or stood before the Sanhedrin for his life. In the marketplace or in prison, Peter, like Elijah, stood boldly for God and proclaimed his word.

A GREAT GATHERING

People attend the Arena Church because it is refreshing and because everything is done on their behalf. It is a people-focused church filled with experience. Large or small, the Arena Church is a great gathering of God's people who love to worship him and love to love one another.

However . . .

Not everyone can take the frenetic pace of the action. It is too loud, long, lively or something like that. Oh, maybe it's great for a Sunday or two, but not for long. Can you imagine Christians who are inclined to "go deep" lasting long in an Arena Church? It can't happen. They would snap like a twig. In fact the Arena Churches only do Bible study to get to the worship service. It is like the *hors d'oeuvres* before the main *entrée*.

Study the checklist below to see if you have an Arena Church, or if you recognize any churches that might fit the Arena style.

CHECKLIST

___ You have had a pageant, conference, or living Christmas tree in the last year.

___ Your worship service lasts longer than one hour and fifteen minutes (please include only the preaching and music).

__ Your pastor moves around in dramatic fashion and gestures forcefully while he preaches.

__ You have a television ministry (or you really and truly want one).

__ Your pastor wears makeup secretly and wants to be in a movie. Ouch! I am really pulling your leg here.

Those who lead or attend Arena Churches are special people. They are some of the most gifted, loving, and authentic people in the kingdom of God.

Chapter 6

THE CORPORATE
CHURCH

The Key: Vision
Pastor as CEO

THIS TYPE OF CHURCH IS GENERALLY LARGER THAN the others because it is complex, intricate, and very efficient. One primary reason for its size and complexity is the nature of the pastor. He is a strong leader, with leadership gifts the rest of us can only imagine. These pastors are unbeatable for motivating large numbers of people to achieve a singular vision. This vision generates all kinds of ministries and activities going on at once, all leading back to the skills of the pastor and staff.

Most men would love a Corporate Church, where the vision and purpose are guided by the strong hand of the pastor. It's his vision. He's firmly in control. A Corporate Church is a purpose-driven church. It's the living, breathing vision of the pastor, who is the CEO of this corporation of believers.

The Corporate Church is complicated and wide-ranging in nature and scope. The reason is that the pastor is complicated and wide-ranging. He can put a lot of balls up in the air and keep them there, just like a CEO keeps up with all the components of a corporation. Thinking of a Corporate Church, you think of IBM, known throughout the business world as Big Blue. And you think of God's Big Blue. Think of a Corporate Pastor you know as he walks into the pulpit—of the assurance that's just a given when he comes in. He's in charge of his church. Everybody knows it, and everybody loves him for it.

The pastors of Corporate Churches are what most pastors (like our friend Jason) dream of becoming: men who articulate the vision, describe the problems standing in the way of that vision, align the resources to meet the future head-on, and then motivate the people to achieve the victory! I get excited just thinking about it. The key word here is *vision*. Something large, not easily attainable, and in a word, great.

A PASTOR, NOT A RULER

The term "Corporate Pastor" is in no way to suggest that this type of preacher rules from an ivory tower, or is unplugged from the issues and concerns of his congregation. A Corporate Pastor is one of the most gifted leaders among all types of pastors. He is a man fully capable of handling complex tasks, keeping many projects running at once, and leading people to accomplish great things in ministry.

These are men who have an extraordinary ability to envision things and to see the "big picture" when others cannot. They are the true strategic leaders, and often lead churches of all sizes to do things which others could not imagine. The Corporate Pastor begins with a view of what God is doing or what the Lord wants done in a church, and then moves to lead his people to achieve that vision.

Corporate Pastors are great communicators because they can see and define a vision for their people in clear, concrete terms. They are great motivators because they can move the hearts of the people of God to join in his mission. And they have the ability to allocate the best resources of people, money, and programs to accomplish what needs to be done. These men come in many personality types, but they share a common ability to get people to gather themselves around a common mission.

TOWARD THE VISION

Corporate Pastors generally do many things very well. They are able to study, preach, build relationships, lead people through complex situations, motivate people to do great things for God, and maintain a healthy and balanced life. It is not unusual for these types of pastors to have hobbies and passions (such as sports) at which they are very good.

Corporate Pastors are leaders of the vision, and they find their greatest fulfillment, whether communicating, writing, preaching, leading, and relating to their people in moving people toward the vision. They lead best by leading others to accomplish tasks of ministries. They enjoy seeing a lot going on at once in their churches, and they seem always to be moving to the next level or the next horizon.

THE RIGHT PACE

There are things that men like these should watch out for, and perhaps the most important is being sensitive to the gifts and orientations of others. The Corporate Pastor can easily become impatient or discouraged with any of his people who do not grasp the vision or direction he sees so clearly. This type of preacher can move too fast, and end up so far ahead of his congregation that resistance can build between pastor and people, causing conflict to break out between the two.

Corporate Pastors also may not understand the single focus of other individuals (such as staff members and other local ministers), or that these people enjoy predictable routines. Corporate Pastors generally feel stifled and boxed in by long-term planning sessions, and may move quickly from idea to idea or dream to dream. In doing so they often leave others in the dust who are still trying to fulfill the last idea or vision that was presented.

Corporate Pastors must always be sensitive to their ability to go faster and farther than the people they lead. They must communicate effectively and take care to stay focused on the visions they have helped to establish for their people. Otherwise they risk leaving them behind.

SOMETHING BIGGER

Many people enjoy the leadership of Corporate Pastors. They like their energy and focus and the feeling that the church is going somewhere with the Lord. They like the articulation of a vision, and the way the pieces are outlined and managed so they fall into place to achieve that vision. Many members of a Corporate Church congregation like the notion that they are a part of something bigger than anything they could enjoy as individuals. Corporate Pastors have the ability to pull people together to form something bigger than themselves.

BIBLICAL MODELS

The biblical characters who remind me of Corporate Pastors are David and Solomon. Both of these men were gifted in many areas and accomplished much in their reigns. David was a musician, warrior, writer, leader, and administrator. Solomon was a writer, national leader, builder, and developer of Israel. Each man had the ability to do an amazing number of extraordinary things simultaneously and with seeming ease. Corporate Pastors are like these two. They do many things well with ease.

However . . .

Not everyone is charmed by the vision of the pastor and the demands of the Corporate Church. Who wants to be compartmentalized? Who wants to be put on a base (what if I strike out?), in a ring (crowd, congregation, committed, core—Elton Trueblood, where are you?!), on a path, or in a designated position in a big organization? Who wants to work for Big Blue or GM during the week and come to God's Big Blue on Sunday?

Who wants this? . . . Thousands and thousands of people across the U.S. and around the world. They love the crowds, the vision, the organization of it all. They love the leader, the complexity, the feel of something big happening.

Study the checklist below to see if you or your church qualifies as a Corporate Church.

CHECKLIST

__ Your church has a vision/purpose statement that is prominently displayed.

__ You have seen an organizational chart of the church-staff relationships.

__ Decisions are made by a few, and you like it that way.

__ Your pastor has autographed photos and books of Rick Warren and Bill Hybels.

__ Your parking lot areas are named after geographical places in Scripture like Zebulon, Naphtali, and Caanan (I'm not making this up).

__ The elders just voted to issue an IPO (initial public offering of stock). I'm out of control here, but watch for it just in case.

Don't be mistaken. There are many Corporate Churches out there, and they come in all sizes. There are many pastors who have incredible leadership gifts in this style. But can you imagine what a pastor who wants to lead like this finds when he goes to serve an Arena or University type of church?

Keep reading. There are more interesting comparisons ahead.

Chapter 7

THE MACHINE CHURCH

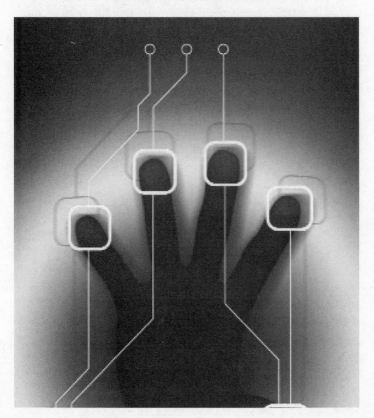

The Key: Programs
Pastor as Manager

THERE IS NO SUBTLETY HERE. THE MACHINE CHURCH is just what it appears to be. It is a well-oiled, well-operated, well-functioning machine. The key word with this church is *task*. Do something. The pastor is the boss, the foreman, the manager. Visions can wait, worship is later, doctrine is assumed, but nothing can be more important than what is to be done.

The focus is on programs. What are we doing here today? What do we need to do? Just tell us what to do. The pastor frames the problem. Machine Churches love problems. We've got to have problems. What's the next problem? Is it the steeple? Is it the pig that needs barbecuing? We've just got to get these people mobilized. A lot of Southern Baptists are proud members of Machine Churches.

THERE'S WORK TO DO

The pastor here is kind of a sergeant going around checking up on the troops hard at work in the trenches. There's no TV broadcast, no tape ministry. Media in the Machine Church is nonexistent. Who needs it? We've got work to do here. Who needs to go deep in the Word when there's so much work to keep us occupied? The Lord's calling is all around us. We don't have to look it up.

Let's build a Habitat house here—come on, let's go! What's next? How about this Sunday School program? It's the well-oiled machine, getting a squirt of oil here and a new part there, and just running on day and night. For the Machine Church it really doesn't matter what the task is; it can be painting the church or having a barbecue. Just get the work assigned and do it. Things need to be done and done right now!

The pastor of this church is great at discerning what needs to be done and pointing it out to his people. The specialty of the Machine Church is programs, programs, programs!!! Nothing is more important than programs, emphases, and seasons because they point to and direct the people to the tasks to be accomplished.

Machine Pastors are the hardest-working pastors in the kingdom of God. They are activists by nature, and they have an inordinate ability to marshal the efforts of people to take on enormous tasks. These men are the managers of the kingdom resources. They are the best program leaders and ministry builders, and they inspire their churches to roll up their sleeves and get it done. These are the pastors who never stop looking for the tasks at hand, and they work faithfully with great feeling and effort to accomplish those tasks.

SEE THE POTENTIAL

Machine Pastors excel at managing the start-up and operation of programs, ministries, and organizations. They have great ability to see the potential of people and lead them far beyond where they themselves can imagine going. They have an affinity for hard work and great challenges. They are the pastors who can build the greatest buildings, lead the greatest mission efforts, and stay at a task until it is finished.

The Evangelical world has been largely built through the leadership of Machine Pastors. They have pioneered the efforts of churches and denominations for years, and have left legacies of great congregations who work, sacrifice, and achieve for the Lord. They have taken the gospel around the globe, built hospitals, children's homes, and universities. These preachers have seen the Great Commission as work to be done for the Lord, and they have built their identities around the work they did.

As one Machine Pastor told me once, "There are only two questions we must ask. One, 'What is God doing?' and two, 'What does he want done?'"

You can look at any church and quickly determine the presence and influence of a Machine Pastor. Is the church well organized and functioning? Are there one or two programs which are the focus of the entire church? Are there major projects that the church is undertaking which excite the pastor and congregation?

GOD'S PROBLEM SOLVERS

Machine Churches love problems. They're God's problem solvers. The pastor leads, the people work, and the jobs get done. Nothing gets them spiritually fired up like a crisis.

One pastor told me an interesting story. He said, "I had to finally get the men of our Disaster Relief Team together in a room and say, 'Quit praying for tornadoes! I'm not allowing you to do this any more.'" They'd watch the Weather Channel, sitting there with their foul-weather gear within arm's reach. Then a report would come on and they would say, "OK! Tornado in Kansas! Let's go!" And they'd fire up the big diesel out back and head off.

I can just imagine them with their big rig, the field kitchen ready-hot. Baked beans on the shelf and the wienies frozen—just ready to go out there and do some disaster relief. These people were doing their work in the name of the Lord and making whatever sacrifices they needed to—including risking their lives. They are essential for building God's kingdom.

ROOM FOR ONE MORE

Machine Churches always have room for one more program. I've seen churches that found out, to their dismay, that another church had a program they didn't have. The first question is: How quickly can we get one started? The next one is: How could we make ours better than theirs? Should we take a course or get certified in something? Should we get a police scanner? Let's get up and running because there's work to be done! (The Y2K scare was tailor-made for Machine Churches. They had Y2K committees for five years.)

PASTOR, FOREMAN, COACH

Machine Pastors are often great preachers and communicators but are not of the same ilk as University or Corporate Pastors. While the latter types often spend great amounts of time preparing for sermons, the Machine Pastor prepares for other things. He is interested in motivating people and moving people forward to the objectives that have been established. Machine Pastors, great men of God that they are, remain so focused on the tasks, programs, and projects that their sermons serve as the communication to keep everyone and everything on track to accomplish the mission. They're like a foreman at a factory or a coach in athletics who stays close to the team or the work crew and pushes them forward to accomplish the work.

Machine Pastors can be impatient with people who cannot follow at the pace required to accomplish the work. They can also misunderstand those who are not by nature hard-working activists. The standards set by Machine Pastors are often impossible for others to attain. Their energy, competence, drive, and focus can be too intense for some of the mere mortals they lead. This type of minister must learn to lead all types of people, and be willing to wait for some of them to catch the dreams and goals he has.

It is a joy to follow a Machine Pastor when things are right because you always know where you are going and what you are supposed to do. Their ability to focus on the important things is refreshing. You do not waste time with useless discussion, evaluation, and processing with a Machine Pastor. You do not have to wonder about the next dream, vision, or flight of fancy. These men are consistent, focused, and powerful leaders who lead others to accomplish much in the kingdom of God.

TASKMASTERS

The Machine Church forms the backbone of many denominations. If we didn't have them, we'd never have the kind of programs we need to build the kingdom of God. Members of a Machine Church will be twice as committed to tying on a nail apron and getting their hands dirty as the people in the University or the Corporate Churches are. Or the Arena Church. In the Arena Church members can get away with being marginally committed because the focus isn't on them, it's up front on the stage. In the Corporate Church, somebody just sort of take cares of it. The University congregation is on another wavelength completely. But in the Machine Church, you either grab a skillet and start cooking, or you'll find yourself elbowed out of the kitchen.

PUTTING THE PIECES TOGETHER

Now the pieces of this whole book are starting to come together. You see, if you're a University Pastor and you're pastoring a Machine Church, you'll keep beating your head against the wall trying to get the congregation to go *deeper,* and they'll keep pulling you by the sleeve just as hard trying to get you to go *farther.*

Big conflict, isn't it? But if you know what kind of church you have and what kind of pastor you are, you can start making the changes you need to make. It's not a matter of being a good pastor or a bad one. University Pastors are just as good and just as important in God's plan as Machine Pastors. It's a matter of being the *right* pastor for the church you lead.

NEHEMIAH'S MACHINE

To me the biblical character that best represents this type of pastor is Nehemiah. Nehemiah built the walls in Jerusalem with an unparalleled focus and determination. He would not stop working despite the threats of his enemies. He understood what he wanted to do, he organized the people to do the work, he motivated them to do something no one thought was possible, and he got the job done. Nehemiah also worked alongside the people and set the standard of work, vision, and focus for everyone around.

God loves the Nehemiahs and Machine Pastors, and he keeps raising them up to lead his people to do great and mighty things.

However . . .

Who wants to labor like this all the time? Who wants to be prodded, cajoled, pushed, and led to work hard? After all, by the time the workweek is over and the lawn has been mowed, aren't we too tired to work like this? I mean, who has the time to be a part of this kind of Christianity? Isn't this kind of commitment out of date and out of style?

Not on your life. The Evangelical movement is built on churches with this style. While others are dreaming and casting pearls before swine (that's biblical, you know), the Machine Churches spin along getting the job done. They will win more to Christ, build more buildings, and go on more missions than others around them.

Use the checklist to see if you know of any Machine Churches.

CHECKLIST

__ You have had a workday at your church in the last six months.

__ You can identify one major program your church emphasizes (for example, Sunday School).

__ You have four equipment sheds out back.

__ Your pastor was in the military and thinks he is a general (but you know he was only a sergeant).

__ Your Building and Grounds Committee is more powerful than the Ladies' Auxiliary. In your dreams, you say.

I wonder what would happen if a Machine Church called a professor-type pastor to lead them? Maybe you've already seen the result firsthand.

Chapter 8

THE FAMILY CHAPEL

The Key: Relationships
Pastor as Chaplain

ALL OVER THE WORLD THERE ARE CHURCHES WHERE folks gather on Sundays with people they are related to or love deeply. Before the service they all spend a lot of time standing around on the steps, in the parking lot, or in the vestibule, talking about the events of the past week, especially if it has anything to do with their children and relatives. Then they go in to church and spend more time together there. The most important thing to these people of God is the powerful force of relationships.

This church is the Family Chapel. The people who belong (and I mean *belong*) to Family Chapels hold relationships sacred. Relationships come before programs, preaching, buildings, and even offerings. Nothing is more important to the people in Family Chapels than relationships.

The people who attend these churches are either related or act like they are. In fact, when it comes to most Family Chapels, you can never really join. You can be born into one or you can marry into one, but you cannot truly join one. You can attend one and belong as a member, but you can't feel a part of the church unless there is a way you can enter through a relationship. The members of Family Chapels have feelings for one another that cannot be described to an outsider.

SHARE THE BURDEN

In the Family Chapel, everybody knows everything about everybody else, because they're all insiders. You can attend it, you can join it, but unless you're related somehow you will never be a part of the *group*, the *family*. And, oh, they sing and weep: "I'm so glad I'm a part of the family of God," (numbering forty-five people at

Mt. Holy Bowl). "I am so glad I'm a part of the family of God. Oh, when we have problems we all share the tears. We just bear the burden together. We're there from birth to death." Lots of heartfelt emotion and sincere love for each other.

A CARING SOUL

If the key word is *relationship* in the Family Chapel, then it follows that the pastor is the Family Chaplain. He is by function (and nature, if he lasts long) a caring soul caring for souls. He is a gentle shepherd, a friend, a guide, a person who understands.

The Family Chapel expects the pastor to be right there in the middle of this big ball of relationships and stay there. They expect him to be *available*—whether that means running off bulletins, driving the bus, or whatever. It's all part of nurturing the relationship. Anything else that's not part of the relationship is better left alone. Every time the old Family Chaplain gets fired up about the Great Commission they fire him—send him off to another deputation. And they get themselves another chaplain who understands their needs.

Now this doesn't mean Family Chapels won't support mission work. They will. And they'll have Vacation Bible School. But pastors who love this kind of ministry more than they love people will never get in through the invisible, impenetrable protective membrane surrounding the membership.

THE RULING PATRIARCH

Family Chapels are usually dominated by a family or two with a ruling patriarch or matriarch who pretty much runs the show. The Family Chapel has trouble assimilating new members and in fact will band together in any crisis, especially those that come against any of the "family." One pastor put it this way, "We grew the numbers with new people, we changed the worship service, we built a new building—and they got a new chaplain."

To repeat myself here, it's all too true that when a pastor gets a hot heart (some would say hot flash) and pushes the people in a Family Chapel on toward more overt pursuit of the Great Commission, he's likely to be headed out the door, with the ruling patriarch engineering (if not leading) the charge.

EYEWITNESS REPORT

I actually pastored the original Family Chapel. In fact, I went back there not long ago for a revival and found them doing really well. The man who was the son of a deacon is now a head deacon up there playing the organ every week. People are born into that church and spend their whole lives there. They always have, and they always will. There's a wonderful sense of assurance and "rootedness" there that no other kind of church will ever have.

During the early part of my ministry there, I was sort of like Jason in that I just couldn't seem to get things right. I was heading in one direction, and the congregation always seemed to be headed somewhere else. One day I was sitting in the living room of a couple. The wife had made lunch for us, and I was talking to her husband. These were godly Christian people, but I simply couldn't understand them. I couldn't figure out where they were going.

REVELATION IN NEEDLEPOINT

Then I looked over and there was a needlepoint cushion on their couch that said "Family Is Everything." And it was like a light of revelation. I thought: *No wonder I can't pastor these people! Family relationships are more important to them than I will ever be or anybody who comes after me will ever be.* They'd had a lot of pastors, and they just expected a lot of pastors to come and go. But the family, and the essence of their worship experience, would continue on like always.

The commitment to family was reflected in the way they made decisions about everything. The way it usually worked was that the patriarchs and their core of advisors all got together and worked out whatever it was, then came and let me know what they decided. We had no business meetings, we had no deacon meetings. Didn't have to. Because the "patriarch committee" made all the decisions.

A BOX OF TOYS

As pastor, I had a box of toys to play in, but I couldn't play with anybody else's toys. I could decide some dates, like when we had revivals and VBS, but I couldn't change the makeup of any of these programs.

One issue I remember was whether or not to have a nursery. Naturally, they loved the idea that families should worship together and that the children shouldn't be banished to the nursery. And so we had them in the worship service—hollering, dirty diapers, and all.

It was no wonder that they asked me to come back for the church's one-hundredth anniversary celebration. I freely admit I am not a Family Chaplain (I'm an Arena guy), but I just learned to accept the fact that they liked those babies crawling all around. And it didn't bother me if it didn't bother them. After a while we all kind of got used to it and thought it was the greatest thing in the world.

A SECRET REVEALED

Once in a while we'd have a visitor with a baby and the child would get to acting up. They'd get up to take them out and I'd say, "Ma'am, don't take that baby out. I can holler over that. We ain't going to be in here that long anyway." And they'd all laugh and punch each other.

In fact, I'll let you in on a little secret. Those babies did bug me. It bothered me because what I had to say from the pulpit was important to me, and I fretted inside over being distracted and upstaged. But having the children there was more important to them, and if I didn't let them sound off, nobody was going to listen.

BUDGET BLUES

I remember one time I tried to set up a budget, and the very idea of it really hurt their feelings. I called a deacons' meeting, and I said I thought we ought to do a budget. I couldn't believe the reaction. All the deacons started crying, "Preacher, are we not paying you enough?" They didn't want to draw up a budget because when they needed money for something they would say, "We got to have a hundred dollars," and take it up on the spot. That's how they did it. They wanted to take care of me—thought they were taking care of me—and I hurt their feelings by trying to draft a budget.

The problem was that I'd been over to a conference at the state office talking about how to be a small church that was really well-run and had all its budget ducks in a row. I think they called it a Small Church Development Conference, and I thought it was a pretty good idea to have one in our church. I figured everybody would like one, and get all fired up about setting goals, establishing a budget, and all that sort of good stuff. But to them it was like I didn't trust them, or they weren't paying me enough. We didn't connect.

BACK TO THE KEY

Some people would say my former church and other churches like it have sort of an old-timey, backwoods approach to things. Amen! It's a wonderful kind of ministry, and it's as vital and alive as any other kind of church. Deep down, a lot of people would like to be members of a Family Chapel. We all want to be with people we like and are comfortable with. We all want to feel we belong.

And that leads us back to the key to the Family Chapel: relationships. Specifically the relationships they *want* to have. Not just relationships with everybody. And so the pastor who's the Machine Pastor or the University Pastor doesn't have a chance. And when all the members want to go on a camp-out over Halloween, and you get on them for that, you are dead meat. Because they want a chaplain. They want somebody to encourage them and their family fellowship, not to remind them there may be something a little shaky about a church-sponsored Halloween event.

BUILDING FOR THE FAMILY

I was talking to some leaders in a Family Chapel one time about a building program. They had plans for a new church with a big door on the side.

"Why do you have a door at the side?" I asked.

They said, "That's for the caskets to come in and out."

And I said, "Well, how many funerals do you have?"

And they said, "Well, we don't have very many, but if we had a door we could have a bunch of them!" Serving the family from first to last.

I also noticed the stage in the plans seemed a little high, and I asked about that.

"Well, the reason we want this stage high is for parents' night at VBS, so everybody can see the kids when they perform."

They had the whole thing figured out. Serving the family was first priority, no matter what the issue at hand.

EXTRAORDINARY GIFTS

The Family Chaplain is both the most beloved and most numerous of all pastors. And let me say I don't use this name to belittle them, but to describe the love and respect they enjoy. There are more Family Chapels in Christianity than any other type church. It's unfortunate that many believers (and maybe some pastors too) discount the importance of these churches, the small ones simply because they are small, and the larger ones because they've built their ministries on relationships and focused on people.

The Family Chaplain is a pastor who has incredible skills in relating to people of all types. He is able to look beyond the behavior of a person, beyond someone's past, beyond the disappointments in their lives, and love them for who they are. These men have an extraordinary gift for mercy toward the people they serve and an extraordinary faith in the God who called them to serve his people. These are the pastors who labor the hardest within their congregations, are paid the least, and have little or no recognition for what they do. These are the men who are often the most mistreated by congregations who do not value who they are and what they do, yet they stay with the work and do it with a resolve and commitment that other pastors can only envy.

THE NEED TO BE THERE

The Family Chaplain is the one who wants (and needs) to be present when a child is born, when surgery is being done, when couples marry, and when a saint passes away into eternity. This man is people-focused, so wherever people gather he is with them. He is the one who receives and returns the most phone calls, visits the most hospitals, knows the most people, and bears the most burdens. He is a man whose life's energy is spent each day caring for people and their needs.

The Family Chaplain will never focus on numbers and resources first. He is focused on people and does not want more people than he can personally care for in his congregation. He wants to know and be known, and it bothers him when there are unknown people in his church.

PREPARING FOR CHANGE

Family Chaplains are generally the most loved pastors because they have such capacity for ministering to people. But they have to resist the temptation to keep the church the way it is. Congregations can change through the years, and it's important that pastors see what's ahead and prepare their people for whatever is coming. Many churches that were once in rural areas are now in suburban areas and need new tools to reach the people the Lord sends their way. Many congregations need training and directions for the future. Some pastors seem almost to dread preparing Family Chapels for change. But the love they have for their people eventually makes them realize managing and controlling change is part of their responsibility to them.

BE PATIENT

Are you a Family Chaplain and not at all sure you're cut out for the job? If you're willing to take the time, you can be a very effective pastor. But you'll do more changing than the congregation will. There's only one of you, and you can adjust your leadership style a lot more easily than your church can adjust its orientation style. If you're willing to do it and will stay with them *long enough,* they will begin to follow you.

You can't do it in a year or two, or probably even three years. You can't take a Family Chapel and turn it into a Corporate Church in three years. If you're a Corporate Pastor you don't even intend to be there that long anyway. You're just learning there. But you can adjust your style to be with those people and to serve them faithfully and well.

JEREMIAH'S FAMILY CHAPEL

The biblical character who reminds me most of the Family Chaplain is Jeremiah. He had the vision of God for his people deep in his own heart, and he ministered to them accordingly. Jeremiah felt the burden of God and the needs of the people in an extraordinary way. He was faithful to proclaim the truth of God even when the people resented him and mistreated him for it. He was an underappreciated, hard-working, sensitive man of God who was used greatly for God's purposes.

EVERYONE'S IMPORTANT

Who would want to be in a Family Chapel? Millions of people! There are more Family Chapels than any other kind of church. People want to be involved in these churches because of the richness of the relationships. In the kind of world we live in, with its frenetic pace, Family Chapels are places of true refuge. They are places where everyone is important to everyone else. They are places where children, youth, and adults intermingle in very healthy relationships. They are places of encouragement and strength. And they are usually places where size makes it necessary for everyone to have a place and a part.

Check this list to see if your church is a Family Chapel.

CHECKLIST

__ Your church has remained the same size in number for the past ten years.

__ You can identify at least one or two prominent families in your church membership.

__ You have changed pastors fairly often and they now tend to be older.

__ You still refer to people as "strangers" who have been members for five years.

__ You have Sunday School classes named after departed members.

__ "Dinner on the Grounds" is more important than Super Bowl Sunday.

I'd better stop.

It's truly a shame that many church growth experts have demeaned Family Chapels. They come in all shapes and sizes and thrive in various locations, but the common thread is that they major in relationships.

So what's wrong with that? Nothing, if you ask those who attend a Family Chapel. In fact, it would be interesting to know the number of people who are now serving in churches as pastors, religious educators, musicians, and missionaries who came from Family Chapels. They are great incubators for the faith.

Chapter 9

THE LEGACY
CHURCH

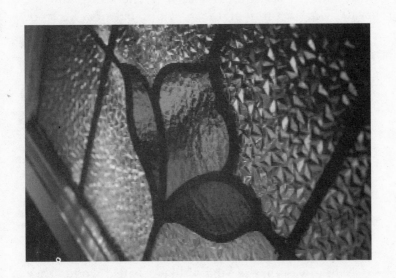

The Key: History
Pastor as Curator

OFTEN THE LEGACY CHURCH STARTS OUT AS SOMETHING else. As a matter of fact, this type of church has to begin as something else or it could never become a Legacy Church. The Legacy Church is forever tied to an event or a person (often a pastor) of larger-than-life significance. In other words, they can never really let go of this significant event or person.

The key idea here is the veneration of history. If they've got "Memorial" in their name, they're on their way to being a Legacy Church. The pastor is the curator, and there's a museum-like quality to everything—to the stained glass, the plaques here and there, and the wall with pictures of the previous pastors. Most of whom didn't stay very long.

And it's never the preacher currently serving who is loved and venerated, it's always the fellow two pastors back. The present minister is just kind of learning to be the curator. This is a church that expects to be taken care of, everything dusted and polished and perfectly preserved.

AT THE CENTER

The Legacy Church is centered around some charismatic personality or cataclysmic event. And these churches have usually been transformed over time from a Corporate Church or a Machine Church or something else. In a way they're kind of like petrified wood. They used to be wood, and now they're gradually getting to be like rock.

Legacy churches are generally adorned with plaques, pictures, and pretty stained glass windows (memorialized, of course). Pastors who served the church are remembered with reverence. There are photographs of them hung along a prominent wall, neatly spaced in sequence, complete with dates of service. In fact, the Legacy Church looks for opportunities to remember significant events, persons, and pastors.

IT'S JUST C. C. POE

I grew up in a Legacy Church that had evolved from a Family Chapel. If you go around that church, you'll see there's a lot of stained glass on the walls in memory of Mama and Daddy. And then there's a plaque commemorating those who served in World War I.

I was back there not long ago, and noticed a plaque set high up on the wall over in the corner of the church. And I thought, *What in the world is that?* And I went over there and it was a plaque to C. C. Poe, who was a venerated church member, a good Baptist deacon, and a guy who owned the hardware in town.

I called a bunch of the older guys over and asked, "Why is this plaque here for C. C. Poe?"

And they said, "What is the matter?"

"Nothing at all," I told them, "I just wanted to know."

They said, "I can't believe you'd ask a question like that. You grew up in this church and you'd ask a question like that? It's there because it's C. C. Poe."

OK. He didn't fight in the World War. He didn't give us a bunch of money. It's just C. C. We just memorialized him.

"I JUST LOVE OUR PREACHER BOY"

First Baptist Churches of anywhere are likely to be Legacy Churches. And if you've got a graveyard within thirty yards of your church and a hardbound copy of your church history, you're definitely in. Also there's usually a particular person whose memory—and whose opinion ("It's what Brother Ralph would have wanted!")—carries tremendous weight.

Years ago I had the privilege of pastoring a Memorial Baptist Church. You could do anything you wanted to today, tomorrow, and from now on if you said something about John Wood, who was *the* venerated pastor in the history of the church. My picture was only two away from his. And his widow was still in our church, so all I had to say was that I talked to Mrs. Wood and she said Brother Wood would be just so excited about this! He'd been dead for twenty-five years, but he would be proud.

Mrs. Wood was in stage three of Alzheimer's. But it didn't matter. I'd gone by the patron saint (or the matron saint), and it was OK. We could do anything we wanted to do as long as Mrs. Wood was on board. And when the discussion would really get hot, I'd invite her to come to committee meetings or business meetings. She'd come in, stand up, and say, "I just love our preacher boy. I really do." Cry a little bit, and then, "Whatever he wants to do, just do it. John would be so happy." It carried the vote every time. But you always had to start with Mrs. Wood if something was important and you wanted to get it done.

THE CULTURAL DIVIDE

As a native Southerner, I can tell you one particularly noteworthy thing about Legacy Churches. You don't get somebody from the states of Northern Aggression and put them in First Baptist Church of anything in South Carolina or Virginia. Part of a Legacy Church is its regional culture and history. Heritage means the world to these people, and they have the bound copies of newspaper clippings and photographs to prove it.

In fact, when I was a youth minister at my home church, somebody said one day that we ought to clean out the storage room and get rid of all that junk. So I did it. And I nearly got *fired* for my trouble. I nearly got fired because I threw away artifacts. I didn't know what they were: chopsticks from Lottie Moon and on and on.

I threw them away, and the deacons had a business meeting over it and said, "We just don't know if we can tolerate this."

And I said, "Well, I'm kind of innocent here."

They agreed, to a point. "OK, yes, you're innocent, but there was a bigger issue and it was the *heritage.*"

They were trying to say, "How do we recapture our precious, irreplaceable heritage that this idiot has thrown away? Artifacts we've been collecting for years and years." And they began to call the saints' names. "What would Vi Harwood say if she knew today that all of the stuff that she so carefully catalogued was *trashed?*" And on and on, and I'm thinking to myself, *Man, why did I do this? I'm just so sorry, I just . . .*

But that's the way they are. "Museum" closets everywhere, plaques and pictures on every wall. These artifacts are what help define them.

A VALUABLE PERSPECTIVE

The pastor of the Legacy Church is a curator in the best sense. He may lead the church to do many wonderful and exciting things, but he must always take care to steer the minds, hearts, and wills of his people around the past to effectively negotiate the present and move toward the future.

The Legacy Pastor is unique in his gifts because he can clearly see the present and future from the perspective of the past. He has an understanding of the past in ways that help him and his people carry out their ministry in the present in remarkable ways.

The Legacy Pastor is at home with the lives and accomplishments of those who have gone before. He has an appreciation for past characters and in fact gains his identity, focus, and ministry style from the past. He is different from the University Pastor in at least this sense. The University Pastor loves to study and takes much from the writings of historic authors, but the Legacy Pastor goes a step beyond that in his appreciation. He seeks to emulate or embody the spirit of great leaders of the past. He wants to be like the Calvins, Luthers, Whitefields, and Wesleys. He sees the heroic nature of great leaders of God and takes up their strengths as a leader.

On the eastern banks of the Jordan River about 850 years before Christ was born, the great and mighty prophet Elijah was taken up to heaven in a whirlwind, and the mantle of his ministry was literally given to his successor, Elisha. Elisha had a fruitful ministry in his own right. However it was built upon, and extended the reach of, the ministry of Elijah. Elisha walked in Elijah's footsteps, taking up his legacy to accomplish what the Lord had given him to do.

Like Elisha, the Legacy Pastor often follows in the shadow of a prominent figure who has gone before, using that predecessor's influence as a tool to continue God's work. He may never rise to the same stature, and may never have everything that the earlier pastor had, but he will find a base in that legacy to build upon. Elisha could never have accomplished what he did had not Elijah paved a way for him. The path he inherited was clearly marked and designed for him; he only had to continue and improve it. He had essentially the same type of ministry as Elijah, but through God's grace was able to take it to a level Elijah never knew.

We find the same lesson in the legacy Jesus left to his disciples: "I assure you, the one who believes in Me will also do the works that I do. And he will do even greater works than these, because I am going to the Father" (John 14:12). The Legacy Pastor is most fortunate to have a way marked and provided to him for an exciting and fulfilling ministry.

THE POWER OF THE PAST

In the front of the Legacy Church you'll often see a communion table. On it are inscribed the words of Jesus, "In Remembrance of Me." On the windows surrounding the sanctuary are the names of bygone saints with the unwritten (but very definite) words, "You had better remember me!" Jesus is more important, of course, but the past is undeniably powerful. The Legacy Church moves at the speed of history. "Never forget!" might be the battle cry for those saints who remain.

Why would anyone want to be in such a church? I mean, who wants to be reminded of history and heritage every Sunday? Many thousands of people. Legacy Churches have rich heritages that should not be set aside just because things change. They are filled with people who know and understand the ways of God in the past. The past can be a wonderful window to the future. Legacy Churches have an irreplaceable role to fulfill for their communities and denominations.

Check out the checklist on the next page and see whether your church has any of the following character-istics of a Legacy Church.

CHECKLIST

___ You have a bound church history.

___ You have a wall of photographs of every pastor who has served the church.

___ You hear words like *legacy*, *heritage*, and *the past* used frequently.

___ You cannot imagine remodeling the sanctuary, much less building a new one.

___ People in the church have pews they have sat in for forty years.

Legacy Churches dot the kingdom landscape, and they are bulwarks of stability in a world of fast-paced change. They are the bedrock of many communities, and their influence over believers is both powerful and positive. The pastors who are fortunate to shepherd these churches have great ministries and do great service in the Body of Christ.

Chapter 10

THE COMMUNITY
CENTER CHURCH

The Key: Issues
Pastor as Prophet

IN EVERY COMMUNITY THERE IS A GATHERING OR TWO
of truly unique congregations. The people of God in
these churches are different from the members of other
kinds of churches. They are activists in the truest and
best sense of the word. Although the Community Center
Church resembles the Machine Church in its activity, the
similarity stops there. Community Centers have a lot of
activity, but nothing that resembles programs and program structures. They are more oriented toward ministries that benefit those in their community, who may or
may not come to the church.

FORGET ABOUT YESTERDAY

The Community Center is a church that lives—
thrives—in the here-and-now. *Today.* Forget about yes-
terday. The Community Center Pastor is a guy who gives
you the theological willies because he's reading maga-
zines and going to R-rated movies to search the culture
and tell you what's wrong with this wretched, wicked
world. He's on the forefront of everything. What he says
may make you wince, but you'd like to say some of it
yourself if you had the courage and self-confidence to.
On the other hand, some pastors would ask why any
man of God would go to *that* movie.

Community Center Pastors spend a lot of time ana-
lyzing. They're always poring over newsletters and political speeches. The congregation is interested in issues
that go far beyond their church. And they're passionate.
They'll get in your face, they'll march on the picket line.

JOE'S BAR

Community Center Churches are always a little on the edge. They're the kind of people who go and witness in bars. "We're going down to Joe's Bar to witness," they say. "Why Joe's Bar?" you ask. "Because that's where the people are. We're not going to wait for them to come to us."

Community Center Churches won't let you witness to people with nicely manicured lawns who live right near the church. No way. They're headed for the belly of the beast.

You'll see some Volkswagen microbuses in the parking lot, and some of the members have been driving the same ones since they joined the Jesus Movement. They started a theological movement in worship away from the intellectual side and right into the middle of the issues and action.

COMMUNITY SERVICE

The Community Center Church is dedicated to meeting the needs and improving the lives of people around the church. It is not unusual for these congregations to have a revenue stream from various sources outside their church or denomination. Sometimes they even administer programs for or get money from governmental agencies. They are God's agents for social and political change that looks toward human redemption. The people in these churches would appear as outcasts in other congregations because they do not fit the mold of the average Evangelical church member. They are out of focus with much of society but very much in focus with the kingdom of God.

Can you think of some Community Center Churches? Ask any of their pastors about his latest sermon series, and he may be a little fuzzy on the details. But he knows how his city councilmen voted on the issues, and knows when they're up for reelection.

Churchwide projects? The community is their project.

A FIGHTER FOR JUSTICE

The pastor of a Community Center Church is prophetic, political, and persuasive. He is a fighter in the best sense of the word. He battles for the souls of people victimized by a society and a world gone wrong. He is savvy, smart, and streetwise. He uses words like *justice* and *injustice* a lot and preaches from the prophets often. He has a keen sense of what people are and what they are not.

Although most of these types of churches are in urban areas, there are examples of the Community Center Church all across the nation. These churches can make ordinary church members uneasy. Pastors of Community Centers challenge other pastors. They are bold, forward, and free-wheeling in their approach to life and ministry, reading books the rest of us avoid and talking in language that makes us nervous.

The prototype Community Center Pastor I always think of is the prophet Amos. He was a man on a mission from God with an attitude to match! He was not a professional prophet (Community Center Pastors loathe titles), but a country boy who had come to the progressive, successful, prosperous Northern Kingdom of Israel with a message and a manner that caught everyone's attention. In the face of a booming economy and high standards of living, Amos systematically thundered a message of judgment and repentance.

He preached against their luxury and extravagance in the face of poverty in the lower class. He was a prophet for the little man and the poor child. He was a champion for the down-and-out and those without hope of changing their lives. He could not rest easy while people starved and were enslaved by their desperate need.

While the rich got richer in the Northern Kingdom, the poor, the widow, and the orphan went begging. Merchants cheated the destitute with dishonest scales, and unscrupulous men stole what little land they had to build their own fortunes. Amos preached against social injustice, oppression, and dishonesty. He was relentless in tracking down those who made their living by usury, slavery, and bribery in Israel's courts.

He also preached against immorality and self-indulgence. The sins of the flesh were as heinous to Amos as the economic and social injustice he saw. While the poor suffered, the wealthy feasted in lavish rooms and sought every sensual pleasure they could imagine. Amos stood as a tower of truth in a decadent city to preach God's word to a hardened audience.

Can't you imagine Amos in your mind? I can because I have known many just like him. They minister in the hard places where life is a risk and things are always uncertain. Their pulpits are strategically placed by God across the cities of our world, and they labor with little or no recognition, reward, or response. But they are champions of the God who called them and sent them to be there. If we are careful to listen to the Community Center Pastors, we may learn more about ourselves and about God than we could ever imagine.

LIFE AS IT IS

Who would want to be a part of such a congregation? Vast numbers of people! These churches are for real! They look at life as it really is and take the gospel of Christ to the heart of some of America's neediest people. These congregations are filled with champions for Christ and true heroes of the faith. They serve the Lord in sometimes dangerous places, with little recognition or earthly reward.

See whether your church has any components of the Community Center Church.

CHECKLIST

__ Your church has more than one community ministry (such as feeding, clothing, education ministry).

__ You have sources of income outside of the gifts from the congregation.

__ You have marched for a social cause.

__ You think people in the suburbs are soft.

Community Center Churches are the vanguard of the kingdom. They are the churches on the front line of the conflict between the world of Christ and the Domain of Darkness. The pastors who lead these congregations don't talk about the fight-they lead it! They have the passion and dignity it takes to rescue people from life's most treacherous strongholds. They are some of our greatest preachers and leaders, even though they are often unknown and unappreciated.

Chapter 11

JASON'S CHALLENGE

LET'S GET BACK TO JASON, OUR EAGER, IDEALISTIC, hard-working young preacher who's on fire for the Lord but frustrated half to death in the pulpit. His head is spinning by now. But he understands that his uneasiness and frustration are legitimate. More important, they're curable—if he's willing to figure out what kind of church he has, what kind of pastor he is, and how the two can fit together. The answers will be crucial to Jason's development as a minister of God, and to his professional success.

FACING THE ODDS

Let's review what he's up against. As a new pastor, he's trying to lead a congregation he hardly knows. They're one of the seven types of churches we've been looking at, with a list of other possible combinations of variables in the mix that we listed earlier. On top of all that, there's the ethnic mix—race, culture, and nationality.

A CONFLICT OF STYLE

Now let's look at Jason's church again for a moment. He's in a small church in a reflective style of worship in a rural area filled with moderate income, working-class people who are high school-educated, politically conservative, theologically moderate, and denominationally fully aligned.

Jason has to factor all of these types and variables on one side of the page, and on the other side he's got to examine the characteristics of his own leadership style. And what does he see? He sees he's not like his church at all. He grew up in a large church with a passionate style of worship in an urban area, and with wealthy parents who were professionals. He's college-educated (post-graduate, mind you!). He is fundamental in his theology, moderate in his politics, and he's loosely aligned in his own denomination.

That's nine significant conflicts right out of the chute. Those conflicts can lead to hurt feelings, stunted professional growth, and general spiritual meltdown. Or, if he understands them, Jason can use his awareness of conflict to slow down a little, look at his ministry, and see what changes are appropriate.

SURVEY THE OPTIONS

He's got to look carefully, though. It is not unusual for pastors to misread the style of congregations they lead. We all have an understanding of what a church is and how it should behave. Unfortunately, many times our understandings are based on incomplete or misinterpreted information, and they lead us to assumptions about our congregations that turn out not to be true. What you have in mind for your people may be far removed from their expectations.

No wonder pastors struggle so much with where and how they should serve the Lord. I actually think it would be a good thing for a pastor, before he goes to a church, to have a little survey among all the adults to find out what their interests and passions are. Not that something like that would determine whether he answered a call, but it would be a part of the decision. Then you see what kind of congregation it is and can say, "I really think God's sending me here," or, "Whoa, God couldn't be in that."

THE ONLY REPUBLICAN

Which of the seven kinds of churches do you think you serve? Which one would you enjoy serving the most? What are your options and opportunities? What can you learn by considering the different styles of churches and your own spiritual gifts? What can you learn from the church where you're serving now?

What I learned at Gober Baptist Church was that I was the only Republican in Fannin County, Texas. Sam Rayburn was the Speaker of the U.S. House of Representatives during Lyndon Johnson's rise to power—he was Johnson's mentor. Rayburn was a legendary New Deal Democrat in that part of the country.

You didn't say anything good about Republicans in Fannin County. It didn't matter how much you loved people, or how often they insisted it was everybody's right to belong to whatever party he wanted to. In practice you'd better be a Yellow Dog Democrat—someone who'd vote for the Democratic candidate even if it was a yellow dog.

I had to adjust my style.

THE OTHER CHURCH POLITICS

Jason is going to have to adjust his style, and it may be a while before he understands that. You have to be flexible. In Fannin County I kept a low political profile. But then when I was pastor at First Baptist Church in Cleveland, Tennessee, most of us were Republicans and the Democrats were in the minority. Many of the elected officials in our community attended that church. Some were Democrats but most of them were Republicans.

Poor old Jason doesn't understand it. He's got a political problem, but it has nothing to do with who's in Washington. He has no idea that he has a church full of roll-up-your-sleeves Family Church people who work hard every day, love fishing, and drive Chevy pickups. Jason wants to turn them into Willow Creek. He understands Willow Creek. He's attracted to Willow Creek.

They can't spell Willow Creek, and they don't care about it.

It's a very basic difference. But if Jason will only stay with them long enough, there's a Great Commission church down in there somewhere that gets on fire and does many, many wonderful things. But they do it as the family of God, not as a corporate body.

DUCKS IN A POND

In every church I ever served I had to adjust my style to the style of the congregation. It wasn't always easy. When I was in a Machine Church, I found that, unlike lots of the people there, I didn't get my spiritual jollies by painting the windows in the sanctuary. But getting things accomplished meant the world to them, and so I learned how to do it. I learned how to pitch in on all kinds of projects and get a real sense of satisfaction from it.

In the Family Chapel where I served, they knew the community. And they knew I didn't know any of that. To me they were all just ducks in a pond to shoot at evangelistically. And they said, "Don't go over there and waste your time on old So-and-So. He's lost, preacher. He's done run every evangelist off." And so I went and talked to old So-and-So, being the hottest prospect I had at the moment. And sure enough, he didn't want to talk about it.

MISTAKEN IDENTITY

They told me, "Look, we don't want you doing this pastoral ministry. Go get us somebody that can do this. You preach and do evangelism and the things you want to do. We'd rather minister to people as a family."

It was a Family Chapel. Underneath the surface they wanted to do something, but they wanted to do it their way. I thought it was a Corporate Church on the surface. My understanding of it was, yes, this is a Family Chapel in some ways, but the Family characteristics aren't as strong as the Corporate ones. I was wrong. So when I started letting them be a Family Chapel again, everything was fine.

I had to change my leadership style, and as a result I was able to describe very specifically to the pulpit committee the kind of pastor they needed to replace me when I left. And they got him, and he is flourishing over there because he preaches and counsels and leads them, and that's all they want.

THE IDEAL CHURCH

Jason thinks that if he tells people about the ideal church he sees in his mind and steers them toward it, there won't be tension. They'll thank him for his vision and fall right in line. But the people understand the church as it is. They like it. They're pretty comfortable with it, even if they know it needs to change. Go to any church and ask any believer, "Are you fulfilled in your Christian life, or can you be more?" and they all say: "We can be more." They can be, but they're happy where they are.

There's a tendency in the young pastor to model himself after others. To realize his vision he copies the mannerisms of pastors who have already achieved a similar vision somewhere else. He goes to conferences and comes back richly blessed. But he also comes back thinking, *I want to be like that guy. I want to sound like that. I want to preach like that.* I've been there, saying, "I want to imitate that guy." But I couldn't do it. Not many imitators succeed. Be content being what God wants you to be, and what he called you to be.

EVERY ONE IMPORTANT

A lot of preachers want the church to grow so they'll look good and be able to climb some ladders. They say to themselves, *OK, here's what you have to do. You'll be here for a while, and then something else will open up, and you'll go to that.* That was the pattern. It's been my pattern at times too.

Maybe twenty years from now Jason will be a Corporate Pastor, which I think can be described as the healthiest type of church. But every church is equally important in God's plan.

Why is the Legacy Church important? Because it tells us where we've been and helps us prepare for the future. Why is the Machine Church important? Because you can't ever get anything done in God's kingdom without a lot of worker bees. Why is the Family Chapel important? Because everybody needs a place to belong.

Why is the Arena Church important? Because we all want to worship God in spirit and kingdom and freedom. You know you can actually lead people there. They don't have to stay with "Rock of Ages" and a piano the whole time. There are other things to see and do in worship. Multimedia is a good thing.

Why is the University Church important? We ought to be sound in doctrine. Why is the Community Center Church important? We ought to be able to read the times.

HOLD ON TO THE VISION

Some pastors want to be at one church the rest of their lives. They make whatever adjustment they have to, but never lose their vision along the way. They get their people excited about that vision, and get them to share it.

It would almost be easier to start with nothing and build a church from the ground up. But 99.9 percent of preachers will never have the chance to do that. They have congregations that keep comparing them to past preachers, and keep shifting in what they want from the man in charge. The church keeps going back and forth—We need a good preacher. No, we need a good pastor! No, we need a leader! No, we need a manager! The pastor is trying to hit a moving target, and in the meantime is probably moving himself trying to find the perfect fit.

But the perfect fit doesn't exist.

Jason must break the cycle somewhere. With steadiness and patience he can do it. By adjusting his style to the style of his people—the people God sent him to teach in his name—he can meet them at their point of need. He can nurture and shepherd them then, and build a strong body of believers who are grateful for his understanding and leadership.

> Here is the key: If you'll take small steps to your people, eventually they'll take large steps to you.

But everybody needs to keep an eye out for potholes in the path.

Chapter 12

BACK TO THE CALLING

THE TIME COMES IN MANY, MANY MINISTRIES— Jason's, yours, and mine—when you're ready to give up. You've prayed and studied and done everything you know how. But you can't get through to your people, they don't understand you, and other opportunities hold only the promise of trading one set of problems for another.

And so late one night after yet another frustrating and unfulfilled day, you decide it was a mistake to respond to the call of the church you're in, and that you've got to figure out how to correct it. Should you quietly put out feelers for a pulpit somewhere else, hoping somehow things will be different there? Take a breather from preaching for a while, to recharge your batteries? Throw in the towel and go sell insurance with your brother-in-law?

WHO'S CALLING?

Keep this in mind: one of the biggest fallacies we have today is that God calls us to churches. That's not what happens. God calls us to *himself*. He sends us to a church, even though sometimes that church is a mess, or we turn it into a mess after we get there. Sometimes it's frustrating because you realize that you and your congregation don't see things the same way. But you're there because God called you to serve him.

If you believe you were called as a minister by God to serve him, and that he placed you in a church to teach his people and build his kingdom, you'll buckle down and serve, even if it means you and your church have to work hard to understand each other. If you believe God sent you to your church, you'll put up with a lot. You'll put up with disappointments and setbacks and attendance problems and financial problems and relationship problems because God sent you there to put up with those things. Maybe even to solve them.

God called Moses and then sent him. He calls you and then sends you the same way.

WRESTLING WITH MOM

When I married, I thought my in-laws were great. I loved them dearly, but their culture was a lot different from what I was used to, and I just couldn't get it. They were more serious than I am. They would laugh, but they would never tell a story. They would never self-deprecate or tease one another. It was almost like you were insulting them if you did something like that.

My family was totally the opposite. My mother and I wrestled until she was fifty-five years old. So you can imagine how my wife's family looked—very proper Mississippians sitting around watching each other swallow—compared with my family rolling around on the floor giving each other frogs, pinching each other, and grabbing each other from behind. Just very loving, showy, uninhibited, touchy-feely, kissing-each-other family. And so when I first met my wife's family I thought, *I'm not going to make it. These people don't like me.*

But I changed my behavior and sincerely came to appreciate them and became very close to them. I had to be like them before they could really appreciate me. Then, in time, they came to appreciate me. My mother-in-law and I get along fabulously now. We're very different people. I can make her laugh now, but only because I was willing to change first.

It's the same principle in a church. If the leader will adjust, then the church will adjust. They will come to you. They will appreciate you for your gifts if you can love and really appreciate them, and really meet them at their point of need. If you take baby steps to them and stay with them, eventually they'll take great strides to you and with you.

SEEING THE DISCONNECT

Not long ago I met with the pastor of a thousand-member church. I had recommended him for the pastorate. My wife and I went out to dinner with him and his wife, and he was so frustrated. He had preached about homosexuals and he talked about people who don't tithe. He is an Arena Pastor. And he wanted his people to come out Sunday night and Wednesday night, and it just broke his heart that they weren't out there worshiping on Sunday night.

His problem was that he was at a Machine Church. His people wanted to work. They wanted something to do, and they didn't understand his heart then. They will one day.

One of the reasons he came to that church was that they set up a very contemporary worship service like the one he'd had at his previous church. The worship leader was up at the piano, and he was a contemporary Christian writer. My friend loved that. He thought the church was just like his old one, only bigger and better, because of the style of the service.

But there was a serious disconnect: an Arena Pastor leading a Machine Church. He was a little bit discouraged because he'd been there three years, and he knew they were following his lead. But guess what? He wasn't leading them to do anything! I asked him, "When you got on to everybody for not attending church, and being homosexuals, and drinking, and not tithing and all, what did you tell them to do?"

His wife laughed and she said, "Nothing." He's an Arena guy—he's a big talker. And he hammered the deep truth of God, and members of that Machine Church wanted to raise their hands and ask, "What am I supposed to do with this? You've been bumping your gums for an hour and I don't know what to do." That's an Arena Pastor. Feel the power. Get to the altar. But he'll leave you a little short sometimes. An Arena guy loves to preach, to experience. But he doesn't always follow through like he might.

Of course, all problems and misunderstandings aren't caused by disconnects between the type of church and the type of pastor. I once met with a pastor who was struggling with a church that wouldn't pay him very much. He was a Family Chaplain in a Family Chapel, but they weren't paying him anything. And I remembered reading in Charles Spurgeon's book *Morning and Evening* that even if the people won't take care of you, God will take care of you.

That's the whole story in a nutshell. Maybe your congregation will take care of you, and maybe they won't. But they didn't call you to preach. God called you. And God will take care of you.

GOD SENT YOU

You may not have a completely fulfilling experience and your church may not be everything you want it to be. But you're there, and God sent you there. And if you don't worry about how long you're going to be there, if you'll make an open-ended commitment, the Lord will really use you. And you'll shape people. By the time you leave, they'll pray like you pray. They'll believe what you believe.

And let me say this to the laymen out there looking for a pastor: don't make your job harder than it is. These are godly men, but they're different. Your church is different. You don't have to match the two up perfectly to follow God's leader. Perfection doesn't exist. But you can use the pastoral changing of the guard to bring about the change that your church has needed for thirty years.

JASON REASSURED

Jason's anxiety is one every preacher knows. But by identifying what kind of church he is in and what kind of pastor he is, he's on his way to resolving that anxiety for good. "You know what?" he might say, "I love these people. And I can minister to these people. And my goal is to train them as believers for as long as God gives me, reaching them in whatever way they need to be reached. Not to change them to conform to my way of thinking." And he matures in the process. And he becomes a preacher his congregation understands. One they feel really loves them and takes care of them in ways they recognize and respond to.

Jason is not a real character, of course, but you're real. Your church is real. And there are real problems and real issues. Real hurts, real disappointments. What do you need to do?

Identify what kind of church you have. What are the dominant characteristics? What are some of its strengths? What's the best characteristic of your membership? What would you change about your folks?

Then identify your strengths and weaknesses as you pastor to these people. How can you best fulfill the Great Commission with them? What is the sweetest fruit you can harvest in the garden you have?

This is not to say that moving to another church is never the right solution. Most of us move any number of times over the course of our careers. But if you look at *why* you're moving, it's likely to be one of the last steps you consider rather than one of the first. And if you do move, knowing what kind of pastor you are, and what kind of church the church you're considering is, you can make the choice that's best for all parties involved.

YOUR SPIRITUAL MILESTONES

One of the most helpful things a believer can do in difficult times is to stop and put down some spiritual milestones. These are memories of times, events, and seasons when God has made himself and his will known in a special, life-changing way. Included in these special memories are decisions you made, people who influenced you, and things that happened to let you know that the Lord was moving in, through, and around your life in a remarkable way.

Each of us has milestones that have made a difference in our lives. Do you remember where you were when the Lord saved you and your life changed forever? Sure you do, and you remember it with ease and great joy. It was a monumental event that has made all the difference in the world. Do you remember the season of time when you fell in love with your wife? Of course you do. To remember it brings the deepest feelings of love for her that you can have. Do you remember the birth of your first child or each child you have? When I do my eyes fill with tears of joy and blessing to think again how I feel about each of them.

Now take a trip back with me to the time and place of your calling to ministry. How many years ago was it? What were you doing at the time? How did God speak to you and what did he say? Were you surprised that he wanted you in ministry? How did you feel to know that the God of the universe had chosen you to be a special servant?

When I go back to the milestone of my calling, I have to go back over thirty years to a small white shingle house in Appomattox, Virginia, on a cold January night. I was a teenage boy listening to a small transistor radio. As a rock-and-roll station played the latest tunes and I watched snow falling outside my window on that night, the Sovereign Triune God spoke to me. It was a definite, unmistakable word that I would preach. I am unashamed to tell you that as my fingers stroke the keys on this computer right now, my tears come unbidden. Each time I think of that night my spirit is moved with joy, purpose, blessing, and a gratitude that I will never be able to express completely to you or to the Lord I love.

I went back to that house a few months ago with a close friend. I wanted to show him where I grew up and lived with my family. We pulled into the drive, and I immediately started thinking about that January night. No one lives there now, so we walked around back. Without thinking, I turned the doorknob, and to my surprise it opened. We walked in and my memories came rushing back. There was the den, the kitchen, the living room where we always put the Christmas tree. I walked down the hall to my old room. The very room where that January night the Lord called me to ministry, to preach. My friend asked to pray for me, and as I stood there on the spot where I lay in bed that night, those memories became another milestone for me.

When the Lord called you to preach, what ministry did you have? What skills did he affirm he would use? Did he tell you each place you would serve and what each ministry would be? No, he called you and me to himself because he wanted us to follow him. The ministries, skills, gifts, and places would come later. It didn't matter, did it? We didn't care because we only wanted to follow the Lord and his call. His word was confirmation enough, and what we were going to do was secondary to that.

When the Lord called me that night, I remember two things vividly. One was saying, "Yes, Lord" to his word that I would preach the gospel. The second was a resolve to follow him anywhere he wanted me to go. The call was definite and the path was open-ended.

Our lives as God's servants have not always led to places of ease and comfort. Some of us have endured hardship to follow the Lord. Some of us have not had the success we hoped we would. Some of us do not compare well in our own eyes to other servants of the Lord we know. We have not been as happy as we thought we'd be. We do not have the church we want, the people we want, or the opportunity we desire.

What we all have, however, is a call from the Living God to follow him and his will for us. We have a call to a life fully devoted to him and fully willing to serve him. Our struggle is not about where we serve or why we serve. It is not a problem of people, location, or opportunity. What is at stake is whether we will build a relationship with the Lord that he desires with us. Your response to the call of God years ago was to give him your life, all of it, because *that was all you could give at the time!* It is no different today. What is required is to give him your life. To exchange it daily for the life of Christ and to live in the power of his Spirit and his Word.

GOD'S MAN FOR GOD'S WORK

Go back to your call. Set a spiritual marker down today and think about what happened then. Recall to memory what you heard and felt there. Resolve to continue the journey and finish it as God wills. Rise above your struggles for a moment and reach up to the One who walks with you each step of your way. He knows your struggles and failures. He knows your frustrations and faults. He has been there when sin overtook you and discouragement fell on you like a morning fog. He knows your unfaithful folks and loves them despite themselves. He knows how you have been treated and how your family has suffered. But preacher, he called you and set you into his service knowing all these things would happen.

You are his man for his work in the place he puts you. Don't let the *where* and *why* you serve a place distract you from the *when* and *what* of your calling. Go with the Lord today without fear! Go with him to the next level of your journey. Your effectiveness today and tomorrow will depend on your relationship with him and little else. Build on that and you will be fine. You are his and he will never forget you. So don't you forget him.

The next time anxiety threatens to get the best of you, or the next time your stomach is in knots, or the next time you wonder how to untangle the knotty problems of the day, or whether you should look for another pulpit, or whether you should even be in the ministry, stop for a minute. Go to a quiet place. And look back.

Close your eyes and try to put in your mind the place where God called you. There's something very powerful in that. What kept me in ministry many days of my life when I absolutely did not know what was going on, was the picture in my mind of a little white house in Appomattox. Each time I go to visit my father, I drive by that house and look at the window of the bedroom where God changed my life. What I may face today or tomorrow may be hard and confusing, but what happened in that room puts everything into the right perspective.

God called me to himself. How could I ever turn away from that?

How Could You? If you were called to preach, you'll stick with it. You can't help yourself. You can't give up no matter how tired or frustrated or broken or confused or mad or hurt you are. The connection between God's call, the pastor, and the love that he has for his people, even when they don't behave wisely, is real and sacred.

As real as your salvation.

EPILOGUE

And so, like John Bunyan in *The Pilgrim's Progress*, I awoke from my swoon and the vision ended. Unlike Bunyan, I was on final approach to Los Angeles International Airport at the time, still experiencing the aftereffects of some unidentified foodlike substance that may have been directly descended from the prison fare Bunyan was served.

But the Lord works in mysterious ways his wonders to perform. However they were revealed to me, I consider *The Seven Churches* Not *in the Book of Revelation* a message worthy of sharing with my fellow laborers in the vineyard, and with any church leader or member interested in improving the relationship and strengthening the spiritual ties between a pastor and his people.

> *For I know the plans I am planning for you—this the* LORD *is speaking. My plans are of peace and not of evil. I will give you a future and a hope. You will call on Me and come and pray to Me, and I will listen to you. You will seek Me, and you will find Me when you search for Me with all your heart.*
>
> —Jeremiah 29:11–13